Training
Your Horse
To Show

Training
Your Horse
To Show

Neale Haley

South Brunswick and New York: A. S. Barnes and Company
London: Thomas Yoseloff Ltd

© 1976 by A. S. Barnes and Co., Inc.

A. S. Barnes and Co., Inc.
Cranbury, New Jersey 08512

Thomas Yoseloff Ltd
108 New Bond Street
London W1Y OQX, England

Library of Congress Cataloging in Publication Data

Haley, Neale.
   Training your horse to show.

   Includes index.
   1. Horses—Showing. 2 Show riding. 3. Horsetraining.
I. Title.
SF295.H26   1975   636.1′08′88   74-30731
ISBN 0-498-01554-8

PRINTED IN THE UNITED STATES OF AMERICA

To
Doug and Jacquetta Mae
whose hard work and encouragement have gone into my books

Contents

Foreword

When Neale Haley first questioned me about being a successful show rider I thought back to my first days with horses. Suddenly it occurred to me that this was a most amazing situation. I had won my first blue ribbon at a Camp Longacres' horse show. And those of us who know Neale are well aware of her close association with the camp. In fact it has been the young riders and horses at Longacres that have inspired her many wonderful books. Now I, a former camper, find myself working with her on this latest book. It made me wonder. I certainly had learned a lot since those days. How had it happened?

I had always loved horses, and had always had an insatiable desire to learn more about them. From the time I received my first pony I worked hard, feeding and grooming him as well as riding. It was more important that he looked shiny and clean than that I did. I read books, asked questions, and listened to what others, especially my teachers, had to say.

It is the knowledgeable and generous people who have helped me learn what they know that has brought me success. And if you really want to become a super rider you must work with the best trainer you can find, and you must believe in him and listen to him. Even the most natural of riders will be better for lessons.

But being a great rider takes more than having a good teacher. It means knowing yourself and knowing your horse. It means recognizing his shortcomings and yours, then confronting them. This process can only be achieved through long hours of practice, and much preparation for competition. There is a lot of work and detail involved. Your first horse show will teach you that the requirements are essentially the same for all shows. You must present yourself and your horse to the best of your ability. You must have show appearance. This means that your horse and your equipment are clean and neat, that your clothes and his tack fit properly. You must have confidence that you will win, but if you don't, you must accept defeat graciously. For the real art of riding—its rhythm, its beauty, the coordination of horse and rider, the pleasure of the horse working hard for you because he enjoys his work, not because you make him work—these are the rewards you come to value. You see the beauty of riding for itself, not just for the prize won in competition.

This book is based on the concept that riding is an art and that to be a competent rider, to be an artist, you must learn to know yourself. It is also a book based on the correct learning of the skills that it takes to be a rider. Perhaps the book's greatest merit is that it is readable and interesting for young readers, and yet based on the sophistication and fact that they will encounter in the show world. It can start you off, smooth the way a bit, and when you become a good rider, still be a companion as it takes on more and more meaning. You can grow in the show ring, and a good book grows in value at the same time. But in the end, your horse, and you yourself, will bring you to value the best moments of the show world.

Tibby Hunt

Acknowledgments

Everywhere in the show world you mingle with great people. Some are great because they have reached the top and become famous. Some are great because of their stature as people. But they all have a quality in common: humility. It is difficult to realize this when you walk about the show grounds; all those regal-looking riders on tall horses give you a sense of inferiority, but just talk to them and you discover what really lies behind showing. These riders are the first to admit that every show teaches them something new. They accept their mistakes and live to correct them in the next class. This makes them excellent teachers. Wherever I have gone to take photographs for this book, I have met such riders. Much of their wisdom is in these pages.

Occasionally you meet a rider and instructor who has that unusual gift for imparting knowledge gained from experience in a way anyone can understand. Within what I feel is the "new generation of riders" I found such a person: Tibby Hunt. Tibby is not only an instructor but is a successful show rider herself on her own and her family's horses. She well remembers her first show when she was only twelve.

"I thought I was pretty good," she says. "One gains humility by riding against really great riders who know so much more than you do. That's not all that improves your riding. It is reaching for perfection, too." Those early years were fun years, when she joined Pony Club and did her first teaching. Later she studied with George Morris, with Locke Richards in his clinics in the American Dressage Institute, with Gordon Wright, and with Victor Hugo Vidal. Three years in succession she qualified in the Maclay and the AHSA Medal classes. In 1967 she was one of the top ten in the Maclay ride-off at Madison Square Garden. She has competed in Grand Prix jumping events in both the United States and Canada. In 1968 she won the Canadian Horse Show Medals final at the Royal Winter Fair in

Toronto. The same year she won the Lieutenant Governor's Trophy for the Buffalo International Horse Show Medal at the Buffalo International Horse Show. In 1969 she was also on the winning team at the North American Prix de Ville Junior Jumping Competition. Tibby Hunt has done judging as well as showing. When I interviewed her for this book, she was riding at the Buffalo International Horse Show, and I caught her between classes. Her advice crops up throughout the book, and I wish to thank her deeply for the care she took to express her thoughts so that they would help other riders, and for the time she took passing it along to me—and to you. I am most appreciative for the time Tibby took to read and comment on the book.

Others among the new generation of riders are Philip and Vicki Ake, from the Ox Ridge Hunt Club in Darien, Connecticut. Philip trains the horses; Vicki teaches the children who ride them. Both bring a vast background of experience to the work. Philip even spent some time at Gladstone, New Jersey, in the tryouts there. His special interest is Three Day Events. Vicki began her riding near her home in Connecticut, at the New Canaan Mounted Troop, and started her showing career on their horses. Her climb toward the top of her profession as a riding instructor began when she went to Ox Ridge Hunt Club in 1968. It was there that she met Philip. He is now manager, which imposes a wide range of duties on him from buying horses to training them. In chapter 11 on Equitation, the series of photographs are of two horses that he has trained. Each of the young riders has been taught on her horse by Vicki. The comments Vicki and Philip made on these photographs are based on intimate knowledge of the horses. To anyone interested in showing, this is a vital chapter.

When I looked for experts to give that added bit of advice that comes from experience and teaching, among this new generation who have all benefited from studying themselves with the "greats," I chose one other who has a special interest in teaching youth: Tom Kranz, director of Longacres Riding Camp, which was founded by my parents. Tom has carried the riding program into the show circuit where Longacres horses are making a name for themselves. But even more important to Tom is the fact that his riders—in the junior divisions at shows—are also doing well. His own show career began late, but this has given him an advantage in teaching. He knows exactly what it feels like to begin showing. Some of the things he is experiencing are translated here with the freshness of new insight and the wisdom only years and intelligence can bring to learning. Tom has studied with Hugh Wiley, which has added depth to his background. You will find his viewpoint most helpful.

Page after page here teaches by photographs. Most of them were taken at two A-rated shows, one in the East at the Ox Ridge Horse Show, the other in western New York at the Buffalo International Horse Show sponsored by the Saddle and Bridle Club. My deep appreciation goes to every rider at these shows who so graciously gave permission to have his or her picture used in a book on showing. These are not "faked" pictures, but taken during the action and tension of horse show classes.

I am grateful to the Ox Ridge Hunt Club for letting me use their facilities and making arrangements with their instructors for me to photograph horses there, and to the Saddle and Bridle Club, who enabled me to take photographs at their show. I appreciate Teddy Wahl's cooperation for always making it easy for me to take photographs at his stable in Greenwich, Connecticut. Ray Moloney was also most cooperative. Janet Offenhauser, manager of the New Canaan Mounted Troop, made it possible for me to take some final shots that I needed on one of the hottest days of the summer.

My thanks go, too, to many others who posed for pictures or helped me get together horses and riders to illustrate particular points in the photography of showing. These are: Mary Reams and Martha Reams Maynard, Nancy Pierce, Betsy Ritchie, Leslie Castle, Susan Glenn Ziegler, Debbie Totten, Penny Tolson, Molly Shearer, and the riders at Ox Ridge Hunt Club.

This book would not even have been born were it not for the background information that came from Kim Haley, who has the unique ability to observe what is going on behind the scenes and in the show ring and then can *put it into words*. She has trained many show riders, trained and ridden show horses, and the feeling of what it is like is woven into these pages because of her. In addition, she put her knowledge of jumping to use with her artistic talent to give examples of fences and especially of hunt courses and training courses.

I wish to thank Mr. Tom Brede for his judge's card—something that is difficult to obtain. His is such a fine example with full detail, it will mean much to those who study it.

*Training
Your Horse
To Show*

PART I

Preshow Training

The show world—a dream can be a reality if you have the horse and the patience to attain it. *Photo by Bob Foster.*

1
Your Riding Style

The happy look of confidence marks the rider who has learned to ride correctly. The look of a winner lifts his head, and communicates to his horse a flowing movement and relaxed eagerness. Sometimes I remember Joyce as a little girl, with a child's thrill about horses, and her tingling excitement at finally being allowed to ride. She had the natural ability that makes riding a joy. Within eight weeks she had leaped from the ranks of beginner to the top class at her stable. But even she, with her thrill still shining in her eyes, never expected the blue ribbon at her first show. Sometimes you are fortunate. You have the natural seat, the gentle hands, the agile body that makes your riding style excellent from the start. Yet it is something that can be learned, too, no matter how late your years or how long you have ridden, or how little.

YOUR FEET AND LEGS

A natural seat helps. But correct form can be instilled in your muscles until they wouldn't dare get out of place. It may seem strange to you, but a good position begins with your feet. You stand on them, so to speak, even when riding. Your feet and legs are the base of your balance. So keep them under you. The ball of your foot is your own balance point. You don't walk tiptoe and you shouldn't ride tiptoe. Only when the ball of your foot is on the stirrup is it easy to keep your heels down. As soon as the stirrup slips toward your toe or home to your heel, your foot position slips, too. Usually your heels go up. But your foot also affects your leg. While your heels are down—and pressed out from the horse's sides—your thigh muscles are pressed close to the horse. This locks you on.

Your legs should touch your horse all the way down his sides. Don't tuck your ankles or heels around him, however. Your legs must swing back slightly from a perpendicular line or you won't have your balance on the balls of your feet. As soon as your legs go forward, your weight shifts back, and throws off your position as well as interfering with your horse's ability to use his hindquarters freely. It is pretty important, therefore, to compare pictures of yourself with the ones here to be certain your legs are in the right place.

If your legs are in the correct position with knees and ankles flexed and the ball of your foot on the stirrup, you can draw a line from the front of your shoulder to the back of your heel.

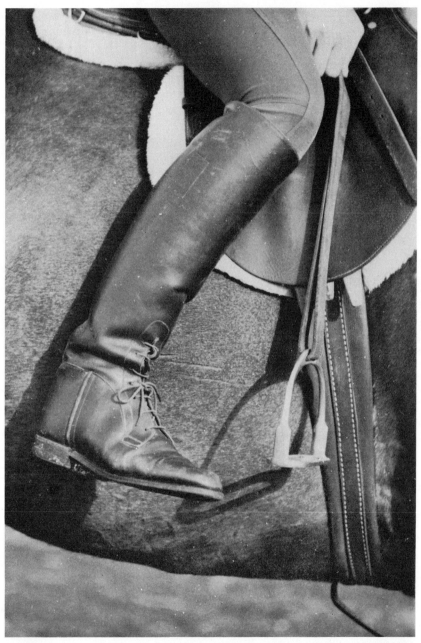

The untwisted stirrup leather, like untwisted, even reins, is one of the little things to watch.

Your stirrups should be long enough to give you a deep, secure seat. Then you can use the calves of your legs with maximum effectiveness. Here the horse is bending around the rider's leg. Your hands must be relaxed, resilient, so you are able to move them independently of your body.

YOUR SEAT

Usually when people speak of a natural seat—such as Joyce had—they mean someone who sits up straight in the saddle. Your back should be straight (without arching) and your head up. Your head is heavy, so that when it tilts forward, it rounds your back and brings your weight forward. An amateur rider or one who is frightened tends to lean forward. This forward tilt is noticeable in a show ring. It won't bring in the ribbons. You need a position of command. Your shoulders will be back, your chin up, your arms dropped naturally at your sides.

Often, when a rider is concentrating, he does odd things with his head or makes funny faces. His head may tilt to the side, or his chin may drop, or his mouth fall open. Watch so that you don't develop any of these habits.

Sit erect and relaxed so your elbows drop to your sides and your forearms touch your body. Your head is up, your eyes forward. Your legs touch your horse all the way down his sides.

Just in case no one ever told you, don't chew gum (or your tongue) either. Don't frown. Keep a happy, pleasant expression on your face.

YOUR HANDS

Think of your hands as if they were something separate from your body, as if they had a will of their own. Your hands by way of the reins are attached to the bit, so, in a sense, they belong to your horse's head. When he moves his head, he should move your hands. Good hands are resilient, soft, "feeling," yet steady and firm. Your fingers and wrists are flexible. They bend easily, remain relaxed. As soon as you notice your hands getting tight, becoming fists, or feeling tense, you have stopped "feeling" the bit.

ALL TOGETHER

Your hands and legs work together. Tibby Hunt, who is not only a top show rider but has often judged horse shows, says that too few riders in classes she has judged know how to move a horse from their legs to their hands. As a judge, she takes this into account when watching a class. If you think about it, you can understand why it is so important. If you ask a horse to go forward, you not only use your legs for leg pressure, but you ease the pressure on the reins. While he responds, he still feels your hands on the bit telling him at which point he has responded enough. This same "working together" of hands and legs takes place at every gait and change of gait.

QUIETNESS

If you were to describe good form in a single word, you would say "quiet." A rider's body is still all the time. His shoulders never move forward and back (even at a canter); his hands never move except in response to the natural movements of his horse's head; his legs never shift or swing.

There's a look about someone who has ridden often in shows. His posture is regal, yet never looks self-conscious. He looks at ease, pleasant, relaxed, yet there is a businesslike attitude about him. He may even seem a bit cocky without showing off. You can imitate this attitude. You can even assume it when you are scared right down to your boots—but it takes practice, lots of practice.

WALK AND TROT

You will find it easy enough to keep your posture erect at a walk, but as soon as you begin changing gaits, you run into trouble. Even at a sitting

Post close to your horse; keep contact with your thighs; let his motion thrust you forward (rather than you standing up). A slight angle to your body is correct for a rising trot.

trot, however, you have to have that quietness in your body. When you post, you must still be erect. Your body must move in one piece. You don't want your hips swinging back and forth while the top of you is going up and down. Let your horse's rear legs thrust you from the saddle forward. But keep the movement to a minimum. You should not rise a dozen inches from the saddle. A lot of practice at a sitting trot will help you feel the forward shove of your horse so that you learn to post lower and lower. Often practice trotting without stirrups to improve your balance.

Debbie, who failed to win in a Pleasure Horse class at a State Fair, was a bit shocked when the judge told her, "You didn't post at a trot." She *had* posted! But her horse had such a soft trot, it didn't *look* as if she were posting. After that she had to "fake it." She rose high enough to let a judge see that the back of her pants left the saddle. But Debbie's experience is a rare one. You are much more likely to post too high by exaggerating the thrust of your horse's legs. If your horse has a rough trot, you will have to "fake it" too, by managing somehow not to post too high in order to make it *seem* as if he has wonderful gaits.

CANTER AND GALLOP

Even at a canter your body remains still. And at a gallop, too. Pumping is out. Watch your legs especially at a canter to be sure they don't move.

STOP AND BACK

When you stop, tilt your head back slightly. Remember to use your

Your position is erect at a sitting trot and at a canter.

If you were lined up in a horse show, waiting your turn to back, you would stand still until the judge stopped behind you. Then you would back straight. Your horse should flex at the poll; he should not open his mouth. His legs must move in diagonal pairs to be correct. Here the rider has her weight slightly forward as she squeezes with her legs to bring her horse into the bit.

hands and legs together. A rider who had often ridden in the jumping division in horse shows became puzzled when discussing equitation classes. "I don't understand this business of leg pressure when you stop," he said. "What do you mean you don't pull on the reins?"

One way to stop a horse *is* to pull on the reins, jabbing the bit back in his mouth and forcing him to stop. It is a lot better to let him stop himself. You do this by using leg pressure to move him forward, but at the same time you keep pressure on the bit. Your horse becomes more and more collected until he seems to ask himself, "If I can't collect any more, what do I do? I have to stop."

You back a horse the same way. Since he is already standing still, the movement he makes in response to leg pressure is checked by the bit so that his movement has to be backward. He should back without fighting the bit. He should flex at the poll without overflexing. His mouth shouldn't open, nor should his head tuck to his chest. There should be a straight line from the bit to your elbow.

TURN

When you turn a horse, you use both hands and both legs. The rein on the inside of the turn asks him to turn his head in that direction. The outside rein checks him enough so that he does not turn his head way out of line with his body. The inside leg presses at the girth so that his body bends around it. The outside leg presses behind the girth to bend his hindquarters. You may say this is just like dressage. Good riding is dressage in the finest sense.

You need to remember that when you turn a horse, you will look in the direction you are going. This will also shift your weight to the inside of the curve. You do not want your body out of line or your position to change. All of the aids you use to ask your horse to turn are so imperceptible that it takes a judge in a show ring to see them. And he is looking for them.

USE A FORWARD POSITION TO FEEL BALANCE

One of the best ways to train your body to quietness and strength is to practice riding in the forward position. This is often called the galloping position or the jumping position. When you first work at it, keep your hands on the mane, and hold it tight. This prevents you from yanking on the bit if you lose your balance. As you get better balance, you can rest your hands on the crest. Keep the reins long for a while so that if you fall into the saddle unexpectedly, you still won't jerk your horse's mouth.

Practice trotting more than cantering. It is more demanding. It will also help you learn to balance more quickly. Turn in circles, make figure eights, stop, take a canter from a walk. When you can do all of these things without needing to use your hands for balance or to catch yourself, you are approaching show ring ability.

Have a picture taken of your position. Be certain your shoulders are up, your head high, and your *heels down*.

The next step is to practice in a forward position with your hands held a few inches out to the side of your horse's neck while you keep contact with your horse's mouth. It is ever so important you do not pull on the bit during this training process. You need to develop a "feel" for the movements of

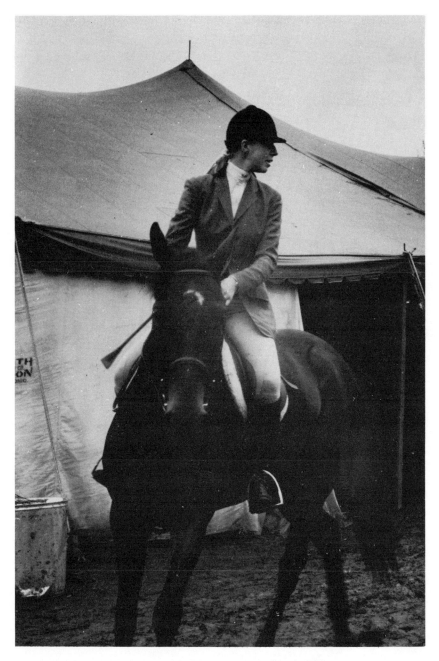

Look where you turn in order to shift your weight slightly that direction and to see where you are going. The pressure on the rein is small. Use leg pressure at the girth on the inside of the turn and leg pressure behind the girth on the outside.

The forward position (rising from the saddle) at a canter will give you balance, train your muscles, and improve your hands better than any exercise. Practice trotting as well as cantering in this position.

your horse's head. Your hands will move forward and back at a walk and a canter, but will be almost steady at a trot. This is because your horse's head moves with his strides more at a walk and a canter; hence his bit moves, so your hands should move. Let the bit pull your hands forward. Feel it. This training will teach your hands to move independently of your body. You must learn to know this touch if you ever hope to be a fine rider.

Always check the girth before remounting even if you're sure there is no need. It is a correct mounting habit out of the show ring or in it.

Take the reins (and the crop) in your left hand before resting it on the crest. The bight should be on the left side. Your right hand goes across the top of the pommel. (It stays there all the time you are mounting.) You are permitted to lengthen the left stirrup before mounting if you are too short to reach it from the ground.

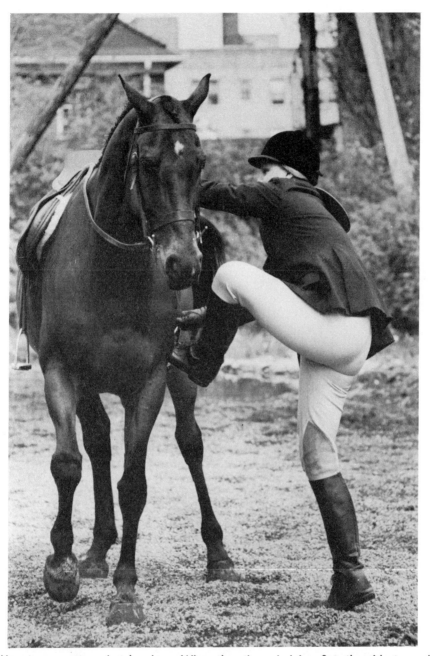

Mount, no matter what he does. When the stirrup is lying flat, the side toward his croup comes out for your foot. Swing clear with that right leg. Sit down easy. Adjust your reins. Then shift the bight to the other side (if you ride with it there). Finally pick up your other stirrup.

When you dismount: shift the bight (and the crop) to the left side so that they don't drag across the withers. With the reins in your left hand, place it on the crest. The right hand rests on the front of the saddle, either above the stirrup leather or across the pommel.

Your leg should clear his back completely when you dismount. Your right hand *does not* shift to the back of the saddle. You want to remain balanced with your weight over the withers all the time you dismount, and you do not want to adjust the length of your reins in the process.

Your weight remains balanced, in the same place, as you shift it onto your hands to take your left foot out of the stirrup. Your thighs rest against your horse, but keep your elbows straight. Drop lightly to the ground with your knees flexed. Take your horse at the bit.

2

Training Your Horse at Every Gait

IS YOUR HORSE SHOW MATERIAL?

A blooded horse such as a Thoroughbred, Arabian, Quarter Horse, Saddlebred, and so forth makes a better appearance in a show. That's not all. Usually a blooded horse has the build and stamina needed to win. What if you own a cold-blooded horse, one who isn't anything special except to you? Of course you can show. Neighborhood and stable shows give you a chance to get experience and even to win ribbons.

A pony can be shown in Pony Club shows, 4-H Club shows, pony shows, and even in shows where most of the contestants ride horses. Don't think a pony is an inferior animal. Horse shows recognize how smart ponies are—a pony only has one green year of showing, and horses have two.

The way your horse or pony moves and how well you have trained him help determine if he is show material. I remember watching April school her pony. His joy in life was jumping. Nothing, not even April, could stop him once a fence had been set up in front of him. With a bit of practice, he could enter jumping classes and compete with the best of them. But watch out if April wanted to go in hunter classes, or a pleasure horse class. An all-out gallop wouldn't win there.

If your horse just isn't good enough to show, does it do any good to work with him? It certainly does. *You* learn that way. Who can tell when you might get a chance to ride a real show horse?

Sue Bell, a camper who had taken home a horse for the winter, was only twelve. Her horse wasn't going to win a lot of ribbons, but Sue worked her head off learning everything she could on him. One day, in midwinter, a week before a big show, one of Sue's friends broke two teeth when preparing for the jumping classes. The dentist couldn't fix her up in time for the show. The horse's owner looked around for another rider, tried Sue out, and chose her. Sue had what it took—the courage, the competitiveness, the skill as a rider. Her career on the show circuit had begun.

TRAINING AT A WALK

Showing is work, and your horse must realize it from the start. You know how he likes to spoof sometimes? When lessons begin, he can't do it. Yet you want him happy. The best way to make him like his lessons is to praise him for work well done. And spare the rod.

Keep him perky at a walk. He should step out, take long strides, move along as if he were going somewhere and was anxious to get there. It's nice if he pricks his ears. Should you have a horse who looks sour naturally, don't add to the irritation. If he hates a crop, or spurs, or loud clucks, avoid them.

Walk in straight lines. That sounds simple, but it isn't. A horse will cut corners, meander, do anything he thinks shortens his work. Plot your course, then stick to it.

Steadiness is important. Count the four beats to his walk. The rhythm should be constant, unvarying, never speeding up or slowing down. That isn't as easy as it sounds either.

Suppose your horse is a bit lazy. You can't whack him all the time, nor squeeze all the time. Use leg pressure on alternate sides with each stride to keep his walk perky. If he needs more encouragement, a swat with your crop at the start of the lesson will make him pay attention. If he is slow to feel leg pressure, use a training whip or crop behind your heel *at the same time* as you use leg pressure. Another method is to dig your heel around in tight, hard circles just behind the girth.

Practice turns at a walk. Make large circles and small ones, oblong and conical ones. Reverse toward the fence and by going into the middle of the ring.

Your horse should stay quiet and move along well with loose reins as well as on contact. His circles should be as neat, his turns as responsive, as if you kept a stronger hold on him.

AT A TROT

He should take his trot smoothly. A sudden start means you startled him into it. Always shorten your reins first, just enough to take up the slack that will be there when he tucks his head properly for a trot. If you need more impetus, use leg pressure each time you sit into the saddle.

Reverse: one method is to circle into the middle of the ring and go the other way. Another method is the one used by this rider. Come out from the fence at a forty-five degree angle . . .

When you have enough room to turn around, start back toward the fence as if making a circle so you end up going the opposite direction. Be sure there is enough room for your horse to circle without breaking gait.

His trot should have an even beat. Count the two beats out loud. Listen to the rhythm. In order to keep the beat at the same tempo when you circle, notice how you have to speed up slightly.

DIAGONALS

A horse trots with diagonal pairs of legs: right front with left rear, right rear with left front. You are always posting on one of these diagonals. Lean forward and watch his knees until you learn to feel with which set of legs you are rising and sitting in the saddle. You should be able to feel it, but even in a show you can sneak a look at his shoulder without dropping your head. You should be rising from the saddle when the leg toward the outside of the ring is forward. Never think you are too advanced a rider to notice diagonals. They must be an automatic reaction with you. If you make a mistake in an equitation class, you are out.

Change diagonals by sitting a beat, rather than standing. This lets you use your seat to keep your horse moving well. Practice changing diagonals until you can do it every other step smoothly and easily. Serpentines at a trot give you practice changing diagonals every half circle and staying conscious of your aids to bend your horse at the same time.

FIGURE EIGHTS AT A TROT

Begin at the center. Trot a circle to your right. It should be round, large enough so that your horse keeps his pace smoothly all the way around. Remember the even cadence. Post on the outside diagonal. Be sure to use your legs to bend your horse and your hands to keep his head in line with his body.

At the center make a smooth change to a circle in the opposite direction and change your diagonal unobtrusively. The second circle should be the same size as the first.

When you complete your eight, stop quietly and exactly at the center. Back several steps, walk forward again and stop. Be sure you back straight. A judge in a show may not ask you to back after you finish, but it is good practice at home.

Since a figure eight is a solo performance at a show, you must think of everything you know when you do it. Look relaxed and pleasant. Always start your posting smoothly. If you know your horse is likely to sneak to one side toward the other horses, be ready for him with a rein that is slightly tighter on the inside. I have seen judges who chose their top places by the way riders trotted, rather than cantered, figure eights.

Diagonals: Posting on the right diagonal means you are out of the saddle when the right foreleg is forward. The rider here is posting on the right diagonal. The correct diagonal is the one to the outside of a circle, or the one on the side toward the fence (if you are in a ring).

THREE SPEEDS OF A TROT

A slow trot is a sitting trot. You should be relaxed, your legs should reach deep and quietly at your horse's sides, your hands should be still. The pace will be even, unchanging, on and on. Let your hips move back and forth to absorb the movement, but keep your shoulders still. If you have trouble sitting relax your thighs, lean back a bit, push your stomach out and your hips forward toward your horses ears. Your horse must take a slow trot without the need of your checking him all the time.

You post to a normal trot. Keep the cadence in mind. Feel the distinct difference from a slow trot.

At an extended trot your horse covers more ground with each stride, but he does not actually go faster. You don't want him rushing around the ring. You will feel an extra moment of suspension in his stride as his legs are flung forward. Maintain the extended trot all the way around the ring.

In a show you must think carefully about where you are going, espe-

A sitting trot should have a steady, flowing, forward impetus. You want a quiet seat and to look at ease with your horse.

An extended trot means a longer stride and a moment of suspension between the two beats. The rider here has her horse nicely collected.

cially at more demanding gaits. Other horses can box you more quickly at an extended trot than at a slow trot. At one show a young girl on a striking chestnut horse had caught the judge's eye. In the middle of the extended trot, she got boxed and had to slow down. A moment of unbalance resulted. The judge never looked at her again.

AT A CANTER

You want a steady canter from your horse. He should be relaxed, moving easily, maintaining the same cadence step after step. Use leg pressure to keep him moving steadily. Work him on the rail so that he doesn't associate a canter with barging around the ring. A quiet, rocking-chair canter gives a good appearance in some classes.

Be exact in your figures. If you cut a diagonal from corner to corner, go in a straight line.

Tom Kranz, after instruction by one of the country's leading horsemen, said, "I learned to use my seat to create impulsion. The forward thrust of your seat into the saddle is the best aid to ask for the canter. It is really getting your impulse from the hindquarters." The method works well with one of his jumpers, with another one a weight shift still works best.

If your horse tends to rush, work patiently with him. Canter a short distance, stop, then pick up a canter again. Be firm. If you can't control him with a snaffle, switch to a pelham rather than risk his rushing with you in a show. It is possible to cover up the fact that your horse rushes by circling or going deep into corners, but it is best to teach him quietness.

LEADS

You know on which foreleg your horse has his lead by watching the one that reaches farthest forward. When he circles, his balance is best if he takes his inside lead. This is why you are expected to take the inside lead—the one toward the center of the ring or the center of a circle—in a show.

The Three Beats of the Canter

The first beat of the canter is on the hind leg diagonally opposite the leading foreleg. The first beat here is for a left lead. (The rider's position is good, but she is a bit forward in the saddle.)

The second beat of the canter is a grounding of the diagonal pair—rear and foreleg together. This is beat two of a left lead.

On the third beat of the canter the leading foreleg touches ground and for a moment supports his entire weight. This is the third beat of a left lead. Your horse should take this kind of a quiet, purposeful canter.

Actually, a horse *begins* his canter with the hind leg diagonally opposite the one on which he will lead. He pushes off for his left lead with his right hind foot first. Next two feet touch together (a diagonal pair): the right front and the left hind. (That puts him on three feet for a moment. Then he lifts his right hind foot.) Now he catches his balance with his left front foot—his leading leg. (He'll lift the diagonal pair so that his left front leg supports all his weight for an instant.) When he lifts that hoof, he'll be airborne, suspended, with all four feet off the earth.

This is why you hear three beats to a canter. The rear hoof is one beat, the diagonal two at the same time is two beats, the lead hoof makes the third.

For an instant all four feet come off the ground. This moment of suspension is where a horse changes his legs around to make a flying change. (In this photo you catch the feeling of horse and rider working together. She is gently checking him as she looks ahead for a turn.)

48

Canter departure: a horse should take the canter and the correct lead as soon as you ask for it. He takes it more easily from a sitting trot and when he is circling. Note here how the horse reaches into the bit, lowering his head, as he prepares to canter. He is still trotting, but starting to change the position of his legs.

Your horse should take the correct lead as soon as you ask for a canter. In a show ring, you cannot lean forward to get your lead, nor throw your weight to one side. When my daughter trained Decision to take his leads, he finally learned to do it with leg pressure only on the opposite side to his lead. Now a light touch by his rider gets a canter and the right lead instantly. Later, when training another horse, her dressage instructor showed her to ask for the lead when her horse put down his rear leg on the first beat of the canter. This is more difficult to do as a rider, because you have to feel where your horse's legs are. It is the easier and natural way for a horse to do it.

A friend who was training her horse for dressage said to me, "It took me two years of dressage work before I could feel when my horse actually pushed off with that hind leg for his lead."

You need to recognize your leads as soon as your horse starts his canter. There is no room for error in a show. If he should make a mistake and take a wrong lead, you must correct it at once. If you have trouble feeling which lead your horse has taken—without looking down to check—remember one lead always feels easier to sit to than the other. Just memorize which one is easiest with your horse. You can sneak a quick look at his shoulders, too, even in a show, to be sure the one to the inside is moving ahead of the other.

DISUNITED—CROSS CANTER

A horse may become disunited (also called cross cantering) when he changes leads, or even when his rider shifts his weight while cantering. The first beat of his canter may be with, say, his left hind leg. Then, instead of bringing down his diagonal pair of legs next (the right rear and left front), he will land on the legs on the same side (right front and rear). Now he's in trouble. So he catches his balance with his left front. And you feel it —it's bumpy. In a show you must correct him as you would a wrong lead by either stopping and starting again, or hoping he corrects himself on a corner. Decision, so obedient about taking the correct lead, has a terrible time changing leads quickly. Flying changes are out. His legs get all mixed up. So his rider knows he must stop and start again if he doesn't want his horse disunited.

FLYING CHANGE

A horse makes a flying change of leads at the instant of suspension. All four feet are off the ground so that he can rearrange them in the air and come down on the other lead. Most horses can also change leads in the air coming down from a fence when jumping. More and more show horses are expected to make flying changes.

FIGURES AT A CANTER

Circles at a canter are good practice for your horse, helping him to bend and improving his balance. If you have trouble with getting the correct lead or your horse tends to be one-leaded, circles help there, too. You take a practice circle in jump classes, and usually pick up a canter part way around. Your horse should take his lead easily when he is circling.

When you canter a figure eight, your figure is similar to the one you did at a trot. Be sure both circles are the same size, are round, and are large enough so that he can maintain his canter without breaking. You should learn to make both a simple change of lead—coming back to a trot before changing leads—and a flying change at the center of your eight. Be sure your horse bends around your inside leg and that his head is not pulled out of line on either circle. Maintain the same cadence to your canter from start to finish. It is nice to face the judge when you do your eights, but is more difficult because you don't have the rail of the short end of the ring on which to start your canter. You should also be able to canter a straight line with either a simple or a flying change of leads in the middle of it. Be sure the line is straight. The change of leads should appear effortless.

You want your horse eager, moving well, but "in hand" for a gallop. Rise into your galloping position.

AT A GALLOP

This is just a faster canter. It has four beats because when your horse puts down the diagonal pair of legs one strikes slightly ahead of the other. It feels rougher—so you rise in a galloping position. Always have your horse under control. In show terms, *in hand* means held under control in your hands.

One day I watched a group of riders preparing for a three-day event—their first. The horses felt good. When the time came for a hand gallop in an open field, I found myself holding my breath. None of the riders looked firm and strong, but, unknown to me, they had been galloping there every day for a couple of weeks. Every horse galloped freely, but every one turned and stopped on cue. If you can do this with your horse, you need not worry about his rushing away with you in a show ring.

After your work out, let him pull the reins long for a reward instead of dropping him into a vacuum so he can't feel your touch anymore.

3
Your Jumping Position

JUMPING POSITION

You must be flexible when you jump. There should be spring in your legs. Balance is the key. Your hands need to be soft and feeling to guide and hold and sustain your horse.

The base of your seat and core of your balance rests on your feet and legs. Not only must they be under you, but weight drops down into your heels. The calves of your legs embrace your horse, touching him all the way down without actual pressure. In order to keep your leg back and also keep your heels down, the ball of your foot must rest on the stirrup. Even your head plays a part, because when it is up you not only see where you are going but you keep your balance and keep your back straight.

SAFETY

Always wear a hard hat—one with a strap and that fits—when you jump. Hold the mane while you learn because it keeps you balanced forward. This also gives you practice grabbing it, something even professionals do when they get in trouble over a fence. Just as important, it protects your horse's mouth so that you don't jab it if you lose your balance. Heels down is the other safety factor. This keeps your base of support under you. A rider seldom falls off if his heels are down because he tends to stay balanced when they are. Your horse, too, is protected. If your heels are down and you hold the mane, you cannot fall backward on the saddle and hit his back. The quickest way to sour your horse on jumping is to sit down on him and jerk his mouth, just when he is putting all his effort into going over a fence!

A strong "galloping" position. Heels down, legs touching the horse's sides, ankles and knees flexed as she squats into the saddle, arms dropped at her sides, elbows bent, shoulders back, body tilted forward, head up, eyes looking ahead. A hard tug on her thigh would not topple her into the saddle, nor would the thrust of a horse as he springs into the air for a jump. Her hands are good, working independently of her body. Practice at a trot and a canter, turning, stopping, and starting while in this position. When your balance is perfect and your hands move freely, you are ready for jumping and following through with your hands.

JUMP WITH YOUR HORSE

You rise into your jumping position when your horse's forefeet leave the ground for his takeoff. Your body should be tilted forward at the same angle as your horse's as you go into the air. This means your seat won't get higher than your shoulders. There has to be forward impetus to your movement just as there is in your horse's spring in order to maintain your balance right with his.

Hold your jumping position as long as your horse is in the air. Sit down only after your horse's *hind* legs touch the ground. If you come back into the saddle sooner, you shift your point of balance before he has his feet under him to catch his. If you sit the instant you land, your seat thrusts him into forward action when you actually want him to move off smoothly and relax. Often in a hunter round you will see a rider stand in his jumping

Hands on the mane and heels down are a must until form becomes natural. The rider's position here is excellent.

Always look at a fence as you approach it, even before you turn to take it.

Rise from the saddle with the forward thrust of your horse as his forelegs leave the ground. Look where you are going. Remain in your forward position in the air . . .

and until all four of your horse's feet are on the ground. Even as you land, prepare for the next fence as this rider is doing.

position the entire time. It is one way to avoid interfering with your horse and demands no action on the rider's part—it leaves everything up to the horse. With a well-trained horse and a beginning rider it may be the best system.

Some horses take their cue from their riders. Decision takes off for a fence when his rider rises in the saddle. It is his cue for timing. This means his rider must start into his jumping position slightly before the spot where his horse should take off. If his rider is late getting out of the saddle, Decision gets under his fence.

HOW TO LEARN THE FEEL OF THE BIT FOR JUMPING

Practice standing in your jumping position while you trot and canter. Learn to start, stop, turn, and circle at both gaits. Ride with contact; hold your hands slightly away from your horse's neck so you do not depend on him for balance. When you can do anything on the flat while standing in the saddle and without ever pulling on the bit, when you can feel every

Your seat should never get higher than your shoulders. Your body will have the same angle as your horse's neck. Throughout the jump, your seat will be farther back than your feet. This is an excellent "beginning" jumping position in which the rider keeps his hands on the crest.

The "intermediate" position: hands take support from the neck, but move forward and down slightly. Always keep your fingers together. The rider's position is good, especially her legs and heels.

The "advanced" position: follow through as your horse moves his head and neck for balance over a jump. You will have the "feel" of the bit. The straight line from the bit to elbow is evidence of soft hands and good contact without interference.

movement of your horse's head and follow it with your hands, when you never need your hands for balance so they are completely independent of your body, then you can follow through with your hands over a fence.

HIGHER FENCES

You must have good hands if you compete over high fences. Your horse needs to feel your support on the bit. No matter what odd thing your horse does with his head, you must feel it and keep the touch of your hands

Many riders use a "noninterference" method over large fences. The reins have a loop to them to be sure to give freedom of movement to your horse's head. This is similar to the "intermediate" method, but requires better balance.

intact. A Saddlebred, trained as a jumper, took an advanced rider over fences at one of the large colleges. He did not do well. "You are dropping him just before the fence," the instructor said. "He has the odd habit of pulling his head back for just an instant before he gets airborne. If he loses the feel of your hands, then, he loses confidence for the jump." The reins must never go slack, nor must you ever pull on the bit, to maintain contact correctly.

You must sometimes grip a little with your lower legs to keep from flying from the saddle on higher fences. Your lower leg encourages your horse throughout the arc of his jump.

FAULTS TO AVOID

Toes that stick out are a common fault. Your heels dig in and ride up at the same time. Stirrups that slip onto your toe or home displace your leg and can be unsafe. Your knees get away from the saddle if your toes go out, and this loss of contact means a sloppy jump.

Heels that go up are not only dangerous from the point of view of balance. They usually swing your leg out of position, too. There goes your feel of your horse. You can topple forward on his neck. If your lower leg swings free and easy it won't give you any support at all. This happens if your knee rolls are getting all your weight.

Looking down has two consequences. You can't look ahead to plan for the next jump; you round your back and upset your balance. Besides, you don't want your *horse* looking down to see what you are looking at. Don't look back either. If the bar fell, you'll hear it go, and it's too late to change things anyhow.

If you are late getting out of the saddle, you drag like a weight against your horse's rise. The most you can do then is to lean forward as much as possible to compensate. If you are left behind coming down, you can both hit your horse and even jerk his mouth, about as bad as faults can get. Stiff legs on landing jar your horse and often make you sit back too soon.

Then there are hands. Tight fists, stiff wrists, taut reins make for hard hands. A tight curb rein is a fault, too. Hands that don't give hurt. If the straight line from the bit to your elbow is broken, your hands are either too high or too low. You can break the line with your wrists either by rounding them or turning your fingers inward, neither of which is good. Don't spread your fingers apart; they are fragile by themselves.

4

Training Your Horse To Jump

The other day when I was buying a horse, the man who owned him said, "Do they really teach children to ride at that stable near here? It always seemed to me they put them on plastic horses that automatically popped over the fences. The riders never learned how to make a horse jump." You need to know how to make a horse jump, but when you know, it is going to look automatic.

I marvel sometimes at the way camp horses develop into good jumpers when they have so many different riders. Perhaps, at Longacres, this was because we had a built-in system that did wonders for the horses while the beginners learned. A lot of work took place between empty jump standards—no bars. The horses became pretty calm about the sight of fences. When actual jumping began, the fences had to be kept low indeed so that the riders could practice and practice position without hurting their horses' mouths and backs. This kept the horses willing. A lot of trotting over fences insured control on the riders' parts even while it developed the horses' hindquarters. Work patterns had to be varied to keep the campers happy, but this meant that the horses never became bored, either. This is pretty much the system you will use yourself to train your horse to jump.

TAKING THE SINGLE FENCE

Look at it even before you turn toward it. This alerts your horse that something is coming up. Take your gait and maintain it. If it is a trot, keep it steady and alert, smooth all the way. At a canter, get your lead, and don't speed up as you get close. Approach the jump in a straight line—no waver-

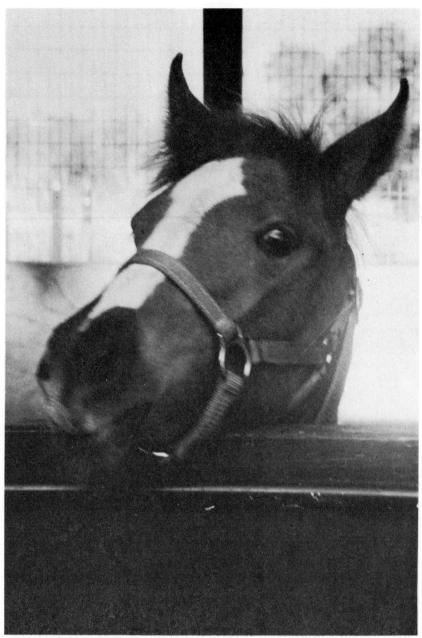

You know you would not train a foal to jump, but a horse should not be jumped either until he is four years old. And then, if it takes you three years to school him to be a good jumper, it is worth it.

When you start training, come straight into your fences. Practice often at a trot. This builds his confidence. It discourages anticipation. It helps get him on his hocks and collect him. It is a good way to help him locate the best takeoff point, because he is able to trot right up to his fence (something he can't do at a canter).

ing, no cut corners. Look up and beyond the fence. If there's a beautiful tree out there, keep your eye on the branches. This keeps your head up and cuts down on anticipation in both you and your horse. The worst thing you can do is start thinking, "We're almost there; we're going to do it. Isn't it high?" Once you reach the fence, rise in your jumping position and hold it until after you touch down. Still look ahead. Maintain the same steady gait. Go straight.

You carry a crop or wear spurs as a reinforcement to your leg aid. (A crop may also be used as punishment for a refusal.) A crop, used correctly, touches a horse behind your leg. Tom Kranz, Director of Longacres, said, "If you hit a horse to get him to jump, he seems to say to himself, 'Now what did I do wrong?' and he forgets all about the fence." But what about those show riders who *do* hit a horse with the crop? "The only time you might use a crop on your horse in a show, other than behind your leg," Tom says, "is after you've really messed up everything. You figure, come what may, you've got to scare him over, and your only hope is a swat behind. So you give it to him, hoping in his horse-mind he'll think someone must be standing there and hit him in back as if to give him a shove."

CAVALLETTI

Basic training is at a trot. This helps collect your horse, and he must be collected to jump well. Try it yourself. Try standing stiff-legged in front of a log and see how high you can jump. Then bend your knees and squat a little. You'll feel the spring. Collection puts spring into a horse's hindquarters.

Begin with four cavalletti raised a half foot that are five to six feet apart. Trot over them. If you are tempted to move them closer because your horse keeps tapping them, you are not getting enough impulsion in his trot. As soon as he trots over in his stride easily, raise the fourth cavalletti to turn it into a low fence. Make it a foot high at first, then work up to a couple of feet. A horse can take fences up to three and a half feet at a trot.

AT A CANTER

The space between the cavalletti for a canter stride will run from slightly over ten to slightly over twelve feet. Watch your horse canter over the cavalletti, then readjust the bars so that he lands exactly in the middle with each stride. Each bar should be raised six to eight inches from the ground. This is one method for determining how long a stride he takes. You can also tell on sandy earth. Or, as one riding instructor said, "I can tell on hot summer days by seeing his hoofprints in the dust."

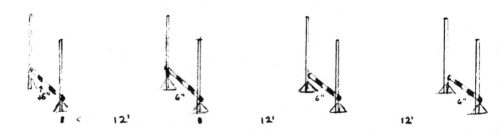

A cavalletti helps a horse judge his stride for jumping.

LENGTHEN OR SHORTEN HIS STRIDE

You can change the length of his stride by lengthening or narrowing the distance between the cavalletti. Keep the distances in his natural stride, however, when you raise the fourth bar for a jump. When you have a higher fence with a cavalletti, remove the bar ahead of the fence and set the first bar on the ground.

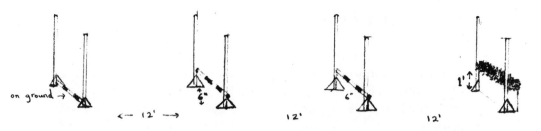

Practice with a cavalletti that ends with a small fence. Keep the bars low, around six inches. As he improves, drop the first of the four bars to the ground, and raise the fourth to make a higher or broader fence.

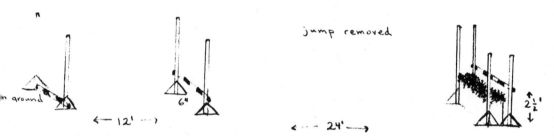

When the fence is raised above two feet, remove the final bar before the fence. This gives your horse an extra stride before he jumps.

LOW FENCES

Work a great deal over low fences. If your horse is in the early stages of training, and often afterward, use the cavalletti along with the jump. Even though you may feel anxious to get to big fences, the low ones are the best training school for your horse. Add a bar to your low jump to change it into a spread. Vary the shape, change the form, conjure up new inventions. It is variety in the fences, repetition, and building of confidence that make a real jumper. In time he must also have a natural extension or shortening of stride, and develop an eye for distance. All of this is best learned over low fences. So stick to it!

A show horse must accept odd-looking fences. This is especially true of a jumper. At one show a miniature painted castle rose its turrets beneath the bar for a fence. That crazy-looking object flustered more horses. So when you think of variety in your fences, use your imagination. Decorate with flowers and flags. Put colored paper on the standards. Take poster paint to some boxes and change the design every couple of weeks. Bring in barrels and bales of straw and tires. Let your horse learn that a new fence is just a curious phenomena of the human race—interesting, but to be jumped.

Often use a cavalletti with your horse when schooling.

Start with a fence about a foot high. Use a variety of fences so nothing new surprises him.

IN AND OUTS, COMBINATIONS

The first time you set up an in and out for a horse you are training, put two strides between the fences. Thirty-six feet is a normal two stride in and out, but it can run anywhere from thirty-one to thirty-nine depending on the horse. Shorten or lengthen the distance so that it is natural for your horse. Begin with a low fence of a foot and a half, then begin to raise the second element. It can be turned into a spread, or a vertical going as high as three and a half feet.

Next make a one-stride in and out. This will normally be twenty-four feet in between, but it can be anywhere from twenty-one to twenty-six feet. Find the natural stride for your horse. You can even set up a no-stride in and out (twelve feet), keeping it low, for your schooling exercises.

Move on to a set of three fences for a combination. Begin with one stride between the first and second fence, and two strides between the second and third. Then switch to two strides in the first set and one stride in the second part. It is wise to keep the first of the three fences lower than the others.

Four fences makes a good set for schooling. If you have a course set up, work over four of the fences for a while, then shift to a different set of four. You can also concentrate your work on three or four fences for a portion of the lesson, then add another and another until you are taking the entire course. You might take a set of four fences as many as ten times for one day's work.

Begin early with an in and out such as this one-stride set.

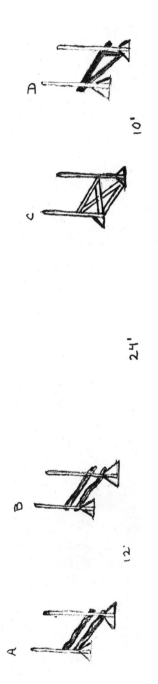

Use a portion of a course, such as four fences in a line, for schooling. (Here you would start with A, B, C, D.) Later in the lesson shift to another set of fences (such as E, F, G). Or you could school over two or three fences, then add a fourth set and finally the entire course. Change the location and sequence of your fences frequently.

71

Set up an in and out with a short stride. A horse does not find this difficult to do if you only shorten the distance slightly at first. You want him to be able to vary his stride easily. Set up combinations with a short stride followed by a couple of natural strides. Next work in a longer stride than your horse normally takes. Avoid setting up combinations of strides that might destroy your horse's confidence. He will find it difficult to take long and short strides in the same combination. You should avoid, for example, two short strides between the first two fences and two long ones between the next two, or the other way around.

Ray Moloney, an instructor at Round Hill Stables in Greenwich, Connecticut, spent an afternoon teaching a green horse with which he had been working how to lengthen its stride for an in and out. This horse always took too short a stride and had to reach for the second fence. Ray set up the first in and out with only twenty feet between. The horse's owner took her mare over the two fences with no trouble. Slowly, a little each time, Ray increased the distance for the one stride. Twice he used a stick on the mare, clucking at the same time. "You expect a horse to obey your voice when you say 'whoa,' " Ray said. "He should respect your cluck when you want him to move on, too." The horse learned to move on. At the end of the hour he could lengthen his stride to take an in and out with twenty four feet be-

When a horse takes off well, he bends nicely, using his neck and head. There should be an arch to his back and neck when he's in the air. The pretty picture is when *both horse* and rider use their skills well, as they do here.

tween. He could even do it in the field and add a fence before and after the in and out with complete confidence.

If you work over combinations inside a ring, work in one direction one day and the opposite direction the next. Somehow this tends to confuse a horse less than altering directions the same day. Put more stress on the lead he dislikes, however. When working a green horse, avoid excessive speeds, because this is confusing to him, also.

HELPING YOUR HORSE TO USE HIS BACK

A fine jumper must extend his neck to use it as a balancing pole, and arch his back. If your horse tends to jump flat, you can set up some parallel bars at the end of your cavalletti. Use a cavalletti in which the first bar is on the ground, the next two six to eight inches high falling within his natural stride, and one stride beyond these, the fence. Make the fence a foot and a half high, but three feet wide. Gradually raise the height and narrow the spread until it gets to three and a half feet high and only eight inches between the bars. This gradually teaches your horse to arch his back while he is meeting his fence in his stride.

TO TUCK HIS FRONT LEGS

Set up a fence with parallel bars a couple of feet wide and two and a half feet high. Increase the spread gradually up to three and a half feet. As you increase the distance between the bars, your horse has to reach more and more for his jump. You can also work to get him to take off early, by a foot or so, so that he reaches for it. Tight combinations, fences with eighteen to twenty-one feet between them, might also help him. When you increase the distance between the bars, you also help him with his hind legs. You can take even longer spreads when you are concentrating on improving his hind legs.

BREAKS AND VARIETY

Jumping should be broken up with work on the flat and relaxation outside the ring. Some trainers even hunt while schooling to give their horses a change of scene.

A horse needs breaks during the showing season, too. You may want to show for one circuit (two or three weeks), and then lay off for a couple of weeks before showing again. A green horse especially should not be "overshown."

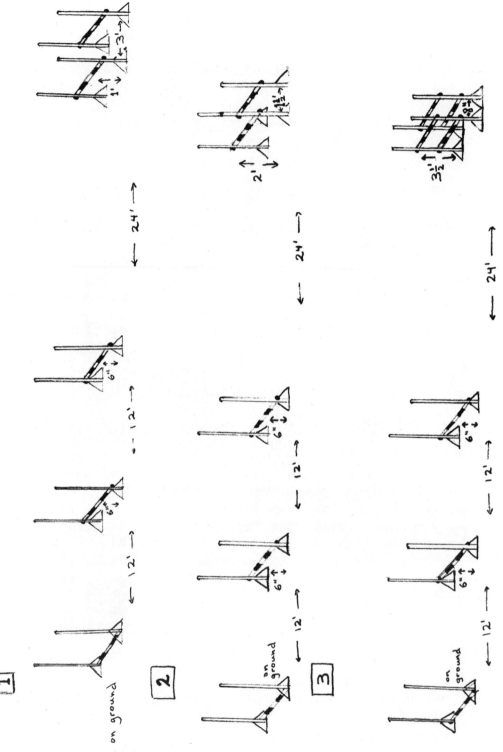

(1) A cavalletti is used before the fence when training a horse to use his back well on a jump. Begin with a low fence a foot and a half high with the sections three feet apart. (2) Next, raise the fence to two feet, but shorten the distance between the sections of the spread. (3) Gradually increase the height and narrow the spread.

Trail rides are one of the ways your horse enjoys most to break the routine of schooling.

HOW YOU HELP HIM TO BE ''ON THE BIT''

A horse who is "on the bit" uses his hindquarters well by bringing his rear legs under him so that he gets impulsion. He responds lightly to your touch, and isn't hanging onto you with his head, yet there isn't a slack rein. You have collection. Trotting over low jumps helps you get it. Simple dressage is excellent.

Circles help. Start with a large circle and, as if tracing an ice cream cone, spiral smaller and smaller, always trotting. Then expand the spiral again. Serpentines and changes of direction keep his attention on you and urge him to bring his hindquarters into action. Don't just trot off merrily for a serpentine. Alter your speed, a fast trot on the long sides, a slow trot around the ends of the loops. Canter sometimes in serpentines.

Trot in circles. Note how the horse is bent here.

Trot in serpentines, extending on the straight away and slowing on the curves. The horse here is on the end of a loop.

Downhill slopes increase the use of his hind legs. When you come across a gentle slope that is free of stones and holes, trot down it. He will have to use his hindquarters for balance. Ride on contact, feeling the impulsion, giving him the sense your hands are there holding him as needed. A steep bank, as steep as he can maneuver—at a *walk*—is another method to use. Never do any work to get your horse "on the bit" unless you are so perfectly balanced yourself that you never need your hands to support you.

THE FEEL OF IMPULSION

Impulsion is forward motion, pressure from behind, spring. It is not speed. A horse needs impulsion to jump. When a professional rider faces a huge Puissance wall, he often takes a hock-gathering stride just before the fence. It is a short stride that draws all the power from his horse's hindquarters.

One day when I watched some girls preparing for three-days events, they were trotting, a couple of horses at a time, between two fences of an outside course. The instructor never gave a hint of warning as to which horse she would ask next to go over the nearest fence. She always waited until the horse she chose trotted quietly, calmly, but alertly. You can practice

Trot up and down gentle slopes to develop your horse's hindquarters.

Take him down steep places at a walk to develop his haunches and balance.

The "feel" of impulsion. Trot in circles beside a low jump. When your horse is going quietly, give him the impulse to take the fence from a trot. You will see it isn't speed in your approach, but "push" from his hindquarters, readiness, that counts.

this same exercise. Only you must not fool yourself. You must take the fence unexpectedly, still trotting, and as steadily and calmly as you were trotting in the circle. You must ask with your legs for impulsion from your horse as you turn to the fence.

CURE RUSHING

Rushing is a form of anticipation. A spirited horse may simply be excited and eager. This type of horse is often an excellent jumper, but it takes a lot of patience to develop him. Adelle Parker, who had toured Europe for forty years with horses, had such a horse—but he sure could jump. When she allowed one of the riders at her school the thrill of riding him, she gave constant advice. "Turn his head to the rail. Don't let him go galloping into his fence that way." Or, "Walk around the corner. Keep calm. Talk to him. Wait. Wait." And then, less than five steps before the fence, she would say, "Now you can let him go." And he would turn into a powerhouse. You are going to have to find the way to calm your "hot" horse if you want to make him a fine jumper. Rushing his fences won't make him time himself intelligently. But you can't walk him into them in a show, either. A good

Trot in a circle that has a small jump in it. When your horse is calm and on the bit, take him over it. Lots of practice with this circle and fence makes him less expectant, less eager to rush.

A horse who is turned aside in front of a fence instead of taking it every time after a straight approach becomes quieter.

rider could take Mrs. Parker's pet horse over a course without rushing, but beginners had to find all sorts of devices to learn the secret.

One method to cure rushing is to set up a low jump less than a foot and a half high within the curve of a circle. Trot around and around the circle taking the small jump each time. After a while your horse ceases to get fussed up over such a little thing.

Another system is to set up a fence in the middle of the ring or in a field where you have room in front of it. Make a straight approach toward it, but instead of taking it, circle to the right or left in front of it. Once in a while, after a calm approach, take it.

A more drastic method is to stop. Make your approach, then two strides in front of the fence, stop. Turn aside and circle. Your horse must learn to do what you ask, when you ask, not what he *thinks* you are going to do. You want him alert and listening to your aids every second. *You* decide whether he is going to jump or not. He must not be able to guess by a shift of your weight, or a lifting of your chin, or a tenseness in your legs, what you intend.

It also helps quiet a horse if you stop after a fence. Canter a few strides only after touchdown, then stand still. Wait a few moments before walking on again.

KNOW HOW A HORSE JUMPS

You have jumped enough now to know that when your horse comes into a jump just right, he takes off in his stride and it all seems easy. You've had times when he had to reach for the jump, or when he took a short stride because he wasn't close enough even to reach for it. You have shortened and lengthened his stride by changing the distance between fences, or by using a cavalletti. You know your jumps depend on his takeoff point, or getting into the right takeoff area so that the jump is an extension of his last stride.

The middle of the fence will be in the middle of his arc.

When a horse jumps, he sets down his leading forefoot in the takeoff area. This is the spot you must notice. His hind feet hit slightly ahead of the spot where his forefeet touched. They shoot him into the air. The height of the jump and even the roundness of the arc are determined by the distance he puts down his hind feet in front of the spot where his forefeet landed.

The takeoff point is usually a foot or two more from the fence than the fence is high. If the fence is four feet high, you'll take off five or six feet in front of it. (On very high fences you may have to take off only as far away as the height of the fence.)

A horse who is well collected will put his hind feet in front of his forefeet to take off. He needs impulsion for this. So your approach will affect how he takes off; it also affects where he takes off. The speed of your approach affects the length of his stride. If you think about it, you know that when you are galloping all out his stride is longer than when you take a rocking-chair canter, which shortens his stride. Three things, then, go into his takeoff: the speed, the length of his stride, the impulsion.

His stride and his speed also affect the arc of his jump. With a short stride (and good impulsion), he will make a rounded arc—a nice half-moon-shaped circle—over his fence. This is what you want for a vertical fence. A longer stride (and good impulsion) gives a flatter arc—the kind he needs for a spread jump.

He will take off in front of his fence at a distance as far away as the fence is high. It will be a foot or two more than this on lower jumps.

Here a horse's hind legs leave the takeoff spot a fraction in front of where his forelegs pushed off. You can see the impulsion the rider has gotten from this horse.

Impulsion is increased if, when you use leg pressure to increase the length of your horse's stride, you hold some of the thrust of his power in your hands. When you approach a vertical fence, you will go slower and steadier. For a spread, you will move on freely, but often with collection in order to increase impulsion. This applies mainly to jumpers, since hunters should meet all their jumps in a flowing stride.

LEARNING TO JUDGE YOUR HORSE'S STRIDE

A single stride of a canter is three beats. You have to feel them. You have to know when he puts down his rear leg to start a beat and when his leading forefoot touches.

As you approach an imaginary fence, or two jump standards without a rail, keep your eye on the takeoff point. See if your horse will step into it with his leading forefoot. Circle at a canter and try again. One stride away —will he hit it? Keep circling. See if you can tell two strides away. You should be able to judge three strides. After a great deal of practice, you will learn to tell as far away as six, but if you can tell even three strides away, you can begin to use your knowledge. The greats among jumpers have an eye for distance. It is a tremendous help. But even if you don't see it right away, keep working, because it can be learned. You can help relax your eye to see distance by relaxing your arms in rhythm with your horse.

Suppose you realize three strides before the fence that your horse is going to be a half stride away from the takeoff area when you get there. He is moving along well, so you feel that if you could get him to lengthen

When learning to find your takeoff point, draw a line on the ground to represent your fence. Canter toward it. See if his leading forefoot hits the takeoff point. Can you tell one stride away if he will get to his "fence" right? Two strides away? Soon you will be able to time your fences. The horse timed this one!

You need to know three strides before the fence whether he can take it in his stride or not. To shorten his stride, steady him as he starts each stride, but maintain impulsion. To lengthen it, use your legs at the beginning of each stride, but hold some of the thrust in your hands.

his stride those last three steps, he'd hit it just right. Perhaps it is a vertical fence, however, and you decide it would be smarter to shorten his stride and get in four strides instead of three. You have to know how to lengthen or shorten his stride.

HOW TO CHANGE YOUR HORSE'S STRIDE

To lengthen his stride—use leg pressure. However, you don't want to let the reins go slack and lose the sense of impulsion. So you will hold back slightly with your hands to cut down on the extension of his forehand. This way you improve his balance.

How do you do it? Feel the first beat of his canter. As he puts down his hind leg to "push off" for a stride, close your legs on his sides. As his leading forefoot touches (and you can see that by watching his shoulder, even if you can't feel as he rocks forward onto it), hold him with your hands. Get a feel for the rhythm of it. Push with your legs on the first beat, hold with your hands on the third. You can practice this without a jump in front of you.

Maintain your own position when you are working on your horse's. Note here the nice line to the bit, the balance of the rider as the horse takes the spread.

When you really do approach a jump, build up the pressure from your legs, more and more with each stride until it reaches a climax with the last stride before the fence.

To shorten his stride—steady him. Again, rhythm counts. You hold him as he takes the first beat of his canter, the beginning of his stride.

Now practice with your imaginary fence until you get the real feeling of shortening and lengthening your horse's stride. Finally, move on to low fences.

There is one other way to change the number of strides between you and the fence. You can take the fence at an angle. This is a more subtle method of altering distances, and involves special work with your horse. For hunter courses and your first shows, you will do well if you can judge your fences and come into them straight for a good takeoff. Besides, you are expected to take hunter fences in the middle.

A horse likes to think he has the initiative. He feels that *he* is jumping the fence. You want him to feel this way so that he develops his own eye for distance, his own sense of timing. If you interfere with his stride right up to the last second of takeoff, you take away the initiative. So, at the last moment, always let him take the jump himself. Then he retains that great sense of confidence that makes for a bold jumper.

5

Courses

HUNTER VS. JUMPER

A hunter is expected to jump smoothly, almost rhythmically. His arc should be perfect over each fence. He should take his fence at a steady pace, time himself well. You want no abrupt changes of speed, no difficulty controlling him.

A rider on a jumper course will constantly readjust his speed, alter his horse's pace, pull up, push ahead when needed, but he still tries to maintain a continuous rhythm. The fences are more demanding than hunter fences are, time can be important, and a spirited, high-strung horse can make a good jumper. A jumper will be able to take his fences at an angle, to lengthen or shorten his stride, take quick turns, and be responsive to a rider's finest aids. Yet many a jumper began his first year in hunter classes. It is a good training ground.

A jumper will need more background in dressage than a hunter. He must be handier. You will work a jumper in tight circles, move from tight circles to larger ones, practice galloping and turning. Many of the things discussed in this chapter apply only to jumpers. You must keep in mind what you are going to demand of your horse on a course, and he needs no more than that.

MEASURE YOUR STRIDE

Learn to take a thirty-six-inch stride—a yardstick long. Practice until your stride is consistent—always the same length. Four of your strides usually

Trot around different types of jump courses without setting the bars in place. You get practice with different courses. Your horse gets practice changing direction and turning.

equal one stride for your horse. On a Grand Prix course, however, a stride is often considered to be thirteen feet instead of twelve, because of the faster pace (hence longer stride) at which it is ridden.

WALK THE COURSE

Begin at the first fence and walk the course in the order in which your horse will take it. Count your strides, "*One,* two, three, four, *Two,* two, three, four, *Three,* two, three, four, *Four,* two, three, four," until you reach the next fence. Then you know how many strides your horse will take if the distance falls naturally within his stride.

Think about where your horse will land after a fence, where he will takeoff for the next one. After a three and one half foot fence, for example, he will land two of *your* strides, or about six feet, beyond it. Look at each fence carefully. Will your horse find that one strange? Be prepared. Plan the direction you will go after each fence, how you will make your turns, which lead you will take before starting the course.

If there is to be a jumpoff, walk the shortened course and think it through. Count the strides on the turns if you will be riding for time, because this is where you can pick up your win.

Walk the course. Count the strides between in and outs and combinations. Plan how you'll ride it. Think about it so you won't go off course. Memorize the diagram by the in gate.

You need a lot of schooling before you are ready for a course like this.

Even if you are riding in a hunter class and feel positive you know the simple course ahead of you—walk it. Linda still feels terrible about the hunter class she entered at an A-rated show in Buffalo, New York. She paid forty dollars, a double entry fee for a post entry, to get into the class. It was very large, so she had to do well to have a chance. Her round was perfect and she knew it. But somehow, in her haste or excitement, walking the course had not drummed it into her head. At the very end, she went off course. One minute she was in the ribbons, the next she was eliminated.

It is good practice to set up different courses at home. Begin simply with serpentine and figure-eight courses, then develop more complex ones. Ride over these courses *without the bars* in place. Soon you will never get off course.

WATCH OTHERS TAKE THE COURSE

You can learn a great deal from other riders. Choose a good rider on a horse similar to your own. You should be able to judge how your horse's stride compares to that of other horses. Watch when a horse about the size of yours, with a stride like your horse's, takes a course.

At one show I sat in a box beside the rail. To my right was a single fence, the first after a change of direction. Four strides away lay the end of

In a hunter course, always take a fence in the center.

the course with a combination that had one stride between the first two fences and two strides between the second and third. Whenever a horse came in too close to the single fence, he had trouble with the combination. He would land too far beyond the first fence, and (since it was the end of the course and most horses were moving out well by then), he wouldn't be able to fit in the four strides before the combination.

Finally, along came a large gray horse, moving quickly, who took the distance between the single fence and the combination in two strides! Now, if you owned a horse who was seventeen hands, you would have watched this gray horse carefully. If he could do it in two strides, so could you. And he would be moving out easily by then so he wouldn't need prodding to get the long two strides in before the combination.

Whenever you watch a show, pick a few good riders and see how they take fences, how many strides they take between them, how they avoid difficult situations. See which fences the horses get "under" by coming in too close to them. There always seems to be a difficult fence that troubles many of the horses. Watch to see how the good riders take that fence. Decide *before* you come into the ring where you will want to shorten your horse's stride and where you may need to lengthen it a bit to take a fence or combination easily. You certainly know you have enough to think about once you get there!

TEACHING YOUR HORSE TO JUMP AT AN ANGLE

Your horse should naturally take his fences in the middle before you begin teaching him to take them somewhere else. Once he takes them in the middle, he should learn to take them at either side when you ask. On a muddy day at a show, it is a great advantage to be able to jump the edge of a fence. The approach may be on solid ground there, rather than slick with the stamp of many hoofs on the beaten path.

The first step in training a horse to jump at an angle begins *after* the fence. Set up a fence no higher than a foot and a half. Go straight over the middle of it. A stride after the fence, turn in a wide curve. When he does this easily, you can begin to take the fence at a slight angle, and a stride after it curve for a circle. Approach it first from one direction, then the other. This will make the angle one way and then the other, always followed by a stride and a circle.

Finally, take the fence at an angle and turn immediately on landing. This is an advanced method of jumping. Never teach your horse to jump at an angle when he is first learning how to jump, because it is dangerous to turn as soon as you land until both you and your horse are perfectly balanced and have had a great deal of practice jumping.

To train a horse to jump at an angle, first take a fence straight but turn a stride after it. Soon you will be able to turn when you land. The next step is to take it at a slight angle. Gradually increase the angle. Advanced show riders are able to get an extra half stride before a fence by taking it at an angle; this is one way to get extra distance ahead of a jump without shortening a horse's stride.

Make good use of your extra hours at a show. Pick out a few experienced riders such as this one, who have the polished, relaxed, "shown often" look. Watch them perform. See why they are always in the ribbons.

As soon as your horse takes slight angles easily, you can increase the angle of the jump, taking the fence at more and more of a slant.

One afternoon when I was taking pictures, an instructor at the stable was teaching riders to turn their horses in the air over the jump. She wanted them to jump at a slight angle and turn to make a curve for an imaginary jump around the corner. In every single picture I took the rider was *looking* where she hoped to go—around the corner—and the horse was turned in the opposite direction. You must use your legs to bend your horse toward the way you want him to turn, just as if you were turning a circle on the flat. Your hands, too, will ask him to turn, one hand pulling him gently into the circle, the other checking to be sure he doesn't turn his head farther than he bends his body.

Your horse is going to benefit by this training. You keep him alert because you keep changing the side and angle of your approach even after you have started toward the fence. He has to keep remeasuring the distance to the fence, and this makes him readjust his stride. He gets more agile as he improves his ability to take off at the right spot.

It is valuable in classes in the jumper division to be able to take a fence at an angle. Not only does it enable you to adjust your horse's strides without altering the length of his stride, it helps him in time classes and in maneuvering on a tight course.

One afternoon Tibby Hunt sat beside me and analyzed some of the jumps on a course she had just ridden. The fifth fence was straight across the ring and looked simple enough, but the sixth fence had been set at an angle. "You have to decide," she said, "whether to take fence Number 5 at an angle so that you can come straight into the sixth fence; or whether to go straight over the fifth one, pull up and make a wide curve to come into the sixth." Since this was a hunter course, a rider would prefer not to pull up if he could help it. "You have to know your horse," Tibby said. "If he falls apart when you jump at an angle, you will want to take the fence straight and go for a wide curve afterward. If he is good on angles, you would take the fifth fence at an angle and go straight into the sixth." She didn't minimize the difficulty of this kind of decision. Analyzing courses is an advanced technique.

"Now there's a good little rider." She pointed to a young boy who had just taken the in and out competently. "He's only ridden three years and is one of those superb riders you come across once in a while. But even the super riders, no matter how good they are, need background. It takes mileage and years to pick up the little things you need to know—there're just so *many* little things."

You should be able to handle a drop jump.

DIFFERENT TYPES OF FENCES

1. A Spread

You will want to take off as close as possible and still be sure your horse will get high enough to clear the first rail. Also, the more freely he is moving, the flatter his arc will be and the farther he can stretch for the fence. A square oxer with the two bars four to eight feet apart is one of the most difficult fences there is. Your horse cannot see the second bar until he is in the air. It is up to you to get him as close as you can to the first one so that his natural arc will be well beyond it, thus making it easier for him to stretch for the second bar.

2. Water

Take off as close to the water as possible. When you are training your horse to jump water, it helps to set up a pole across the middle of it so that your horse understands that this is something to be jumped across, not splashed through. Later you may set up a small fence on the far side to train him to jump all the way across to where the tape will mark the far side in a show.

Square oxers are becoming more common. A high one takes concentrated effort.

On a spread jump a horse flattens out his arc, but must still use his head and neck well.

3. A Bank

If you jump a bank correctly, you will take it the way you do an in and out. One day when I was with a friend at The Ox Ridge Hunt Club in Darien, Connecticut, she pointed to the bank there and said, "We were supposed to go over *that* when we had our three-day trials. No way. My horse said, 'No way.' So did everyone else's." She worried about the summer show, however, which would be an "A" rated show. Her competitors would have wiser horses then.

4. Walls

For a wall or a vertical jump you need impulsion and a short stride during your approach. You will take off as far away from the fence as it is high, plus an extra foot or so. On a four-foot jump, for example, you will take off five or six feet away. With a *high* wall, however, something six feet or more, you will take off as close as six feet from the fence. A horse almost seems to "curl" over such a fence.

5. Downhill

You approach the fence slowly with a short stride. Take off well back in order to land as close as possible on the far side. This minimizes the letdown as you land. A fence that leans toward you on the flat is similar to a downhill fence. A horse often fails to realize the height of it.

If the drop on the far side is steep, you must straighten up when you go over it. Keep lower legs in the correct position. Don't let them swing forward.

6. Uphill

You will approach faster with a long stride. It takes impulsion to jump uphill. Take off as close to the fence as you can so that you don't have to jump any higher than necessary. Stay well forward in your usual jumping position. An uphill fence is similar to one that leans away from you on the flat.

STRIDES AND DISTANCES

Your first hunter courses will have low fences and normal strides between the in and out. Gradually, however, as you enter more difficult classes, the distances get more complex. Your horse will be able to take distances two feet more or less than his natural stride without too much trouble. So if you walk a course and discover that the distance between an in and out is twenty-two feet, you won't worry too much. You know you can shorten your horse's natural stride a bit and make it.

You can expect to find certain types of fences such as post and rails, coops, and, of course, stone walls, on any course. . . .

When you get to jumper courses, you get tough combinations. To take a difficult distance in stride, you may need to take off early for the preceding fence, and thereby gain a few extra precious feet. If you take off too early, however, you will land too close to the base of the first element. Taking off too early can be just as bad as taking off too late or popping the fence.

Speed also enters into your calculations. You get a feel for how long a stride your horse takes at a canter compared to his stride at a gallop. Measuring his speed by yards per minute (say 350 yards per minute as it might

but they will be tougher on a jumper course.

A normal one-stride in and out is twenty-four feet. A normal two-stride in and out is thirty-six feet.

be for a jumper course) is getting pretty advanced until you have had a lot of experience. But you know you can rely on extra speed for a difficult distance in a jumper course. The added speed will lengthen your horse's stride, and if you control him properly, you can increase his impetus as well. Usually, you can negotiate the long distance better by increased impulsion (which is an increase of power) than you can by extra speed.

Say, when you walk a course, you discover that your horse is going to need an extra half stride before one of the fences. How can you get it? You may lengthen his stride between the fences, or you may shorten it for an extra stride. You may take one of the fences at an angle. You may count on pushing your horse into a gallop at that point. You may take the preceding fence short or long to alter the distance. How do you know which to do? It depends on your horse. A horse who tends to flatten out if he reaches for his fences is not the one to push for a long stride and a stretch for his fence, especially if the fence should be a vertical one. If your horse likes to gather himself for a fence and think about it as he comes toward it, you will go for the extra stride. If it is a spread jump, you will probably let your horse move out freely, especially if that is what he likes to do. Your decision will depend also on your horse's stride compared to the distance. He should jump from the point you tell him as long as it is within his capacity to do it.

A Water jump, though low, is long. It can be difficult. *Photo by "Tarrance"*.

A jumper course will have tricky combinations. You may need to walk the distance more than once before you are able to figure out a plan of action. Your plan takes into account whether the fences are spreads or verticals, because this affects your takeoff and landing points and gives you leeway when figuring the number of strides between fences. There may be only one possible way of getting through a combination, and you have to discover what it is. Think of all the alternatives and then choose the one best suited to your horse's temperament.

TURNS

Courses are made up of turns and changes of direction, which mean changes of lead. Smooth turns on a hunter course, smooth changes of lead, help your round. Quick turns, quick responses, can make the difference between winning or not in jumper classes. You can save more time by making sharp turns in a time class than you can by galloping fast. "You have to go fast without rushing your horse if you are jumping on time," Tibby Hunt says, and she knows—she does it enough. "But," she adds, "the turns make the real difference."

Hunter-type Fences

Brush: see A.

In and Out: (may be post and rails, gates, sometimes walls) see B.

Chicken coop: (usually just called a coop) see C.

*Snake fence: see D.

Stone wall: see E.

Gate: (barnyard, garden, picket) see F and H, picket fence is in drawing of a jump course in chapter 4.

Roll top: (the section that looks like half a round coop is usually green) see G. The roll top is found more frequently in jumper classes.

*Bank: see I.

Oxer (natural): an oxer is a spread jump with two sets of standards. In hunter classes it may be built of rails, or a gate and rails.

Aiken: (a glorified brush jump) see M.

Post and rails (natural).

*Railway ties.

*Telephone poles.

*Ditch and fence.

*Less common fences.

A. Brush

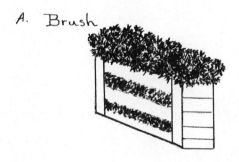

B. In and out of post and rails

C. Coop

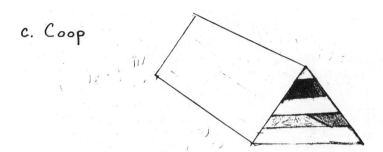

D. Snake Fence

E. Stone wall

F. Gate

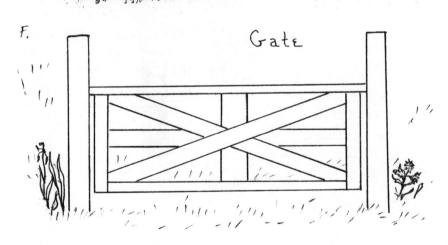

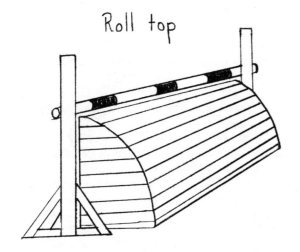

G.

Roll top

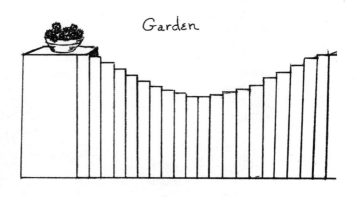

Garden

I.

Bank

Jumper-type Fences

Barrels: see J.

Panel: any type design. See K and R.

Oxer, uneven: a spread with two sets of standards on which the bars are set at different heights. See L.

Water: a small brush jump or post and rails of a foot or foot and a half is followed by a pool of water with a spread of twelve to fourteen feet. See N.

Triple bar: see 0.

Liverpool: a pool of water about five feet wide followed by a vertical fence; sometimes a small coop about a foot high is placed before the water. See P.

Hogsback: a spread in three sections (on separate standards) in which the center is raised higher than the other two bars. Often a barrel or brush is used in the middle. See Q.

X-rail parallel: See S.

Oxer, square: both rails are the same height. See examples in chapter 13.

Any of the hunter type fences may also be found in jumper classes, frequently in combination:

    brush and rails

    gates

    stone walls: see T

    bank and ditch

    wall with gate on top

    gate and rail oxer

    panel and rail oxer (a single rail is often placed on a standard after the panel)

    planks

    roll top

    aiken

J.

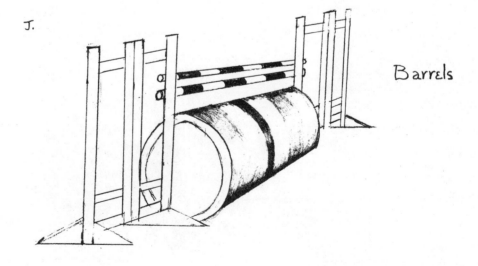

Barrels

K.

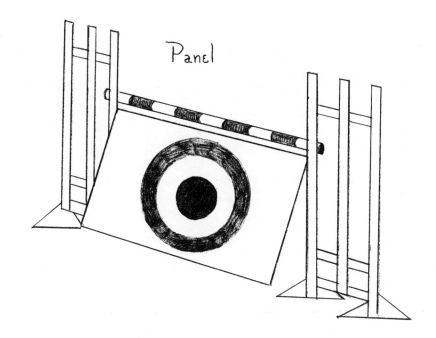

Panel

L.

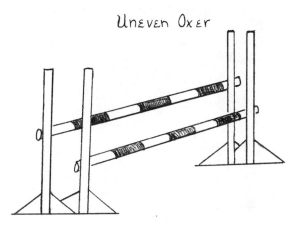

Uneven Oxer

m. Aiken

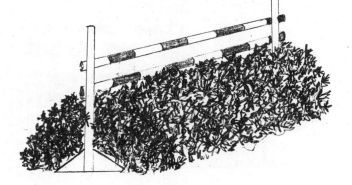

N. Water

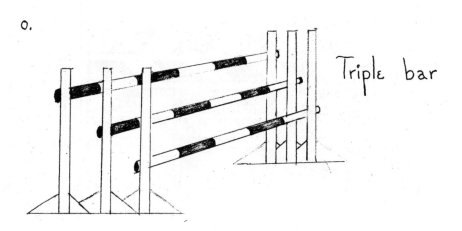

O.

Triple bar

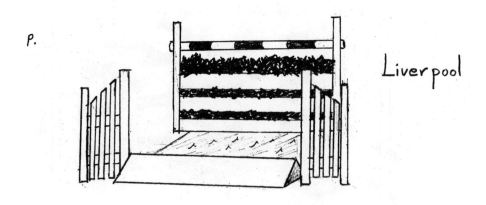

P.

Liverpool

Q.

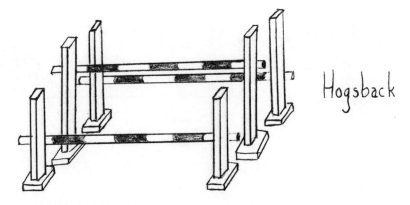

Hogsback

R.

Planks

S.

X-rail Parallel

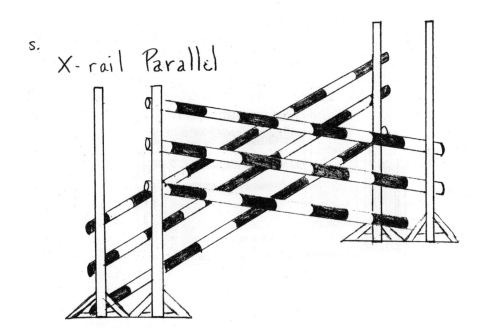

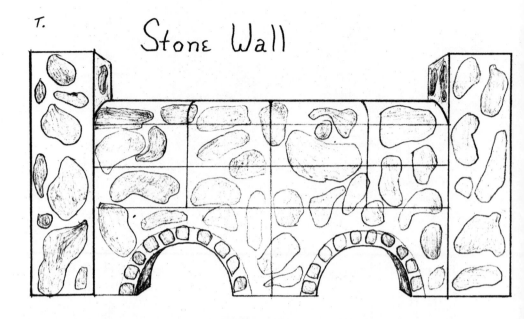

T.

Stone Wall

REST AND BACK TO WORK

A horse gets fed up with routine. When you are schooling, vary the work, mix it up, scramble it, anything to keep the edge on his interest. This means a variation from ring work one day, trail rides another, to schooling over fences the next day. Because horses are creatures of habit, they like to know about what to expect. You will set up a training schedule and stick to the routine. This way you get a natural progression in his work, but can add new ideas and make changes as they are needed. The important thing is to avoid jumping day after day, or the same type of flat work over and over. Even showing gets dull after a while, so he needs a break from that, too. Give him three or four months off in the slack season.

Tom Kranz bought a horse who had gone sour from too much showing. Months passed, but he left the horse in pasture—no work, no riders, no routine. Other show horses went back to work, but not the new one. Wait a while longer, Tom's instincts said. Finally, he risked him in a show. As the horse came toward his first fence, everyone held his breath. A refusal! "Up to his old tricks," everyone said, "too bad." Had the gamble failed? Tom, who is a strong, confident rider, didn't believe it. He rode the horse himself in the next two classes. In both classes, he tied for first (once with one of his own horses). The months of rest had paid off. Since then the horse has been a steady winner. This is Yorke Spring, well known in his home territory because he is such an odd, bungling-looking jumper.

After a horse has rested for a time and you are ready to bring him back, build up to showing gradually. The first three days you might work him ten to fifteen minutes. The following week you would build up to fifteen to twenty minutes, and so on, until he was ready for any kind of work. This is true except in the case of injury. After he had recovered, you would walk him the first week, do some trotting the following week, and then work up to a canter. If the horse is a seasoned show hunter, you may only go a round or two—eight good fences—one or two days before he goes back to the show ring. Some horses, of course, need more jumping practice than that.

Remember, it isn't the hours you put in that count, it is the pressure. It is a lot harder for a horse to go from a slow trot to a canter and back again, or to go from small circles to large ones to small ones again, than to canter up the lane.

"I might give my horse ten minutes of dressage and then a few schooling fences before his first hunter round on the day of the show," Tibby Hunt said of her favorite horse. "Because he is an experienced show horse, he knows what to expect, he is relaxed and he listens readily. It is easy to prepare him mentally, but physically he needs the warmup. An experienced horse doesn't need as much preparation as a green horse. A hunter doesn't usually need as much preparation as a jumper, because his job is more demanding both physically and mentally. You really need to know your horse

Lunge a horse to take the spunk out of him, either before a class or before schooling. *Photograph by Simon Abrahams.*

and what he needs. One horse may get a half hour of mounted work, another I may lunge for fifteen minutes only. Sometimes I warm up a horse for an hour or more before a class, then put him away for a while so he can relax until he has to compete. Sometimes I get on to warm up a horse and get right off again; other times I allow a certain amount of time for a warmup and the horse needs more. It depends on a horse's mood. But if he needs a period of exercise and doesn't get it, you can have a bad round. It's psychological with horses. I come to see more and more how important it is to know the psychology of my jumpers."

6
Faults and Discipline

Most horses love to please. Kindness, praise, and understanding will get the best results. A pat on the neck, a word of encouragement, and a pleased tone of voice are the best praise. Save the tidbits for his dinner. Always try to figure out *why* a horse made a mistake before you resort to punishment. A smart horse knows if a fence is too high and will refuse. A smart rider realizes the reason for the refusal, does not punish the disobedience, and lowers the fence. Be sure your horse knows what is *right* before you punish him.

At one horse show a small girl on a big horse tangled with a white fence. Later in the course, he bungled two more fences in a combination. As she rode out the gate, she didn't look at all upset. "He was just tired," she said. It was the final class, and she was no doubt right.

Often a horse is confused rather than naughty when he disobeys. A rider can give the wrong signal, get unbalanced, many things that add to the confusion. Be sure the mistake is not of your making before you blame your horse.

Punish a horse at the instant of disobedience, no later. Use your crop, your voice, your legs, but don't keep it up. Three or four whacks with a crop behind the saddle are enough punishment. The rider who yanks his horse around, beats him up roughly, and finishes the round in anger is going to be remembered by the judge and the audience. It won't help.

At one schooling show a teenage boy rode a spirited black horse. The first time the horse refused a fence, a loud voice yelled from the sidelines, "Beat him up. Harder, harder." The boy hit the horse on the neck, the back, and finally between the ears. The horse bucked, ran wildly through the rest of the course, and knocked down a couple of fences. The next time

Praise is the way to success in training. Pat him. Tell him what a fine job he did. Note here the carriage of the horse's head, how his neck is bent. He's so obviously pleased with himself.

In a nearly perfect round, he pulled down a bar. "You should have moved him better coming into the fence," her instructor said. You must know why your horse made a mistake in order to correct him.

he came into the ring, many people by the rail turned away, unwilling to watch.

REFUSAL

A rider at an International Horse Show looked dismayed when his horse refused an oxer in the middle of a jumper class. But he sensed fear in his horse, and let him stand facing the fence an instant before taking it again. The horse jumped it. Another rider had trouble with the same fence. He also gave his horse the benefit of the doubt—the first time. When his horse jammed on his brakes for a second refusal, he hit him three times hard behind the saddle. His horse had a clear round thereafter.

After a refusal, hold him so he cannot go forward, and then with the calm poise, the quiet seat you see in the rider here, give him a no-nonsense punishment with your crop—behind the saddle.

Perhaps these riders knew they had taken the wrong pace. Perhaps one of them rode an inexperienced horse, and wanted to build his trust. Perhaps there hadn't been enough impulsion. So the riders gave their horses a second chance without punishing the refusal.

But the time comes when a horse must know he has disobeyed and deserves punishment. Even a green horse must eventually learn to trust your judgment and take strange fences because you have taken him to them.

After you punish your horse, turn in a short circle, give him strong impetus during the approach, and take the jump with confidence.

When you are training a horse and he refuses the same fence over and over again, punishing him won't do any good. Use your head. Compromise. Lower the jump. You want obedience and you should get it somehow so that you win. It never pays to let a horse have the last word.

RUN OUT

Your approach was bad. You may have lacked control. You may not have used your aids correctly. Even so, shying from a fence is a disobedience and should be punished as he does it. The way to correct it, however, is to go back to work on the flat until he is more responsive to your legs and hands. You must feel a horse in your hands as you approach a fence, feel his tendency to disobey. Then you can correct it during the approach with more leg on the side he is thinking about using for his evasion. A quick jerk with the other rein can make him think twice about it, too.

REARING

It is dangerous. Punish him and then cure him. Remember, a horse cannot rear when he is turning, so the moment he starts up, turn him around. Usually he is frightened if he rears, but be forceful about correcting him.

BUCKING

Playful bucking is natural. Horses begin it as foals and high spirited horses never outgrow it. But there is a time and a place for bucking.

At one show a powerfully built horse had a young boy on his back. As they came down from one of the fences, the horse bucked. It was just hard enough to toss his rider forward on his neck. Encouraged by such

A horse who thinks about a run-out can be outwitted by quick action. Here the rider uses her left rein and right leg together effectively.

success, the horse bucked again. That did it. Off he went. And then the horse really bucked, up and down, kicking out his legs, twisting with glee. As soon as someone came near to try to catch him, off he bounded again, bucking as if showing off. Finally, the bucks gone out of him, he let himself be caught, standing as quietly as an old pony. The boy mounted, and took his schooling jump amidst much encouraging applause.

With rain and muck outdoors, the horse had never had a chance to get rid of his excess energy, so he did it in the ring. When you are schooling your horse, turn him out before his lessons so that he has a chance to buck and frolic. Once mounted, you expect him to get down to business. No bucking then. If you have no corral, lunge him.

A friend of mine had a green horse that she was training. He used to buck so hard he nearly threw her off. When he hadn't been ridden for a

A rushing horse can be slowed by using a half halt. It causes him to lower his head and balance himself.

couple of days, he was impossible. A friend told her, "Get off and spank him." It seemed pretty unusual advice, but she was ready to try anything. The first time she dismounted and spanked him, he didn't buck for a while afterward. The second time? He was cured. He never bucked again when she was on him.

DRIFTING

A smart horse may drift to one side before a fence in order to take pressure off a sore foot or to keep you from pulling the bit on the hurt side of his sore mouth. Before you correct drifting as a fault, be sure it isn't due to pain.

Some horses are balanced slightly to one side. (You can increase this defect by always cantering on the same lead or always posting on the same diagonal.) Drifting can also be caused by a rider who has a stronger leg on one side than the other—and he may never realize it.

You must correct drifting on the approach to a fence. One method is to set up an X or an upside-down V with two rails that meet at the top of the fence. When your horse drifts, he will knock himself on these rails until he decides to take the fence in the middle.

If your horse veers to the right, keep the left rein steady and press the right rein against his neck. Use your legs, too. Press your right leg against his side; be sure there's no pressure from your left leg (but do not take it away from his side).

You can also work a horse close to a fence railing or a wall for a while. Keep reversing the direction. Use low jumps so that you can concentrate on feeling him in your hands. You can also try setting up training fences that are lower in the middle than at the sides. He is going to jump where it takes the least effort.

JUMPING TOO HIGH

Young horses often jump fences with room to spare. Don't worry. They will correct themselves soon enough. Horses quickly learn the easiest way to avoid extra work.

FALLS

Hang on to something as you go, if you can, because it breaks the fall. But once you are on the way, let go of the reins. Fall free, and as far from your horse as possible. Learn to relax as you fall because you are less likely to get hurt if you do.

When you get resistance, you need good hands and strong legs to make your aids clear.

PART II

Getting Ready for the Show

7

Show Terms and What They Mean to You

WORDS USED FOR HORSES

GREEN: A horse who is in his first or second year of showing at regular member shows in which horses are required to jump. Equitation classes are also included in green status. The fences must be three feet, six inches, however. A horse can show over fences lower than three feet, six inches, even in recognized shows and not affect his green status. The age of a horse has nothing to do with his being green. A green horse can be three or twenty-three.

Fences for first-year green hunters are three and a half feet. Second year the fences are three feet, nine inches.

You would probably get some show experience for your horse other than at recognized shows before showing him as a green hunter, if he were an exceptional horse. Any horse who has the potential to compete for the championship in Green Working Hunter Horse of the Year Award would be in this exceptional class. Remember that his points are his own and if he is sold, they go with him. Therefore, any showing you do affects his status for future owners as well.

However, if you have a backyard horse you want to show for fun, green classes are a good training ground. You may find some exceptional riders in these classes, but at least the horses will be inexperienced.

REGULAR HUNTER: This can be any horse. His past show experience may have earned him some blue ribbons, and those can restrict what he enters.

QUALIFIED HUNTER: A horse who has been hunted regularly for at least one hunting season with a recognized pack of hounds.

Breeding classes: a horse is shown in hand. This horse, a double-registered Palomino Quarter Horse, wins reserve championship at a state fair.

MAIDEN: A horse who has not won a blue ribbon at a regular member show.

NOVICE: A horse who has not won three blue ribbons at a regular member show in the division in which he is entered.

LIMIT: A horse who has not won six blue ribbons at a regular member show in this division.

In a maiden class the course will be simple with probably only six to eight jumps that are no more than two and a half feet high.

Novice means inexperienced horses in the class. Some of the horses may have shown frequently but have never won enough blue ribbons to get out of the novice status. Fences are lower in maiden and novice classes than in limit or open ones.

The judge will expect more of the horse the higher his status. Not only do the fences get higher as the rating of the class rises, but the courses are more difficult, too.

PONY: A horse or pony who is 14.2 hands high or less. A pony cannot be entered as both a pony and a horse in the same show. Most shows that provide pony classes restrict ponies from entering the junior hunter and other hunter divisions.

TERMS USED FOR RIDERS

JUNIOR RIDER: A youth who has not reached his eighteenth birthday by the first of January the year he is showing. Your age on January first is your show age all year. You will compete against many eighteen-year-olds in equitation classes before the year is over.

P.H.A.—Professional Horsemen's Association. Some of their shows draw the nation's best horses and riders. This horse and rider are in the process of taking a ribbon in a jumper class. *Photo by Wilkinson.*

A junior hunter has the word *junior* in it, so it means people, not horses. It is a hunter ridden by a junior rider. A junior jumper is a jumper ridden by someone under eighteen.

Junior riders may not ride stallions in shows.

MAIDEN: A rider who has not won a blue ribbon at a regular or local member show.

NOVICE: A rider who has not won three blue ribbons in one of these shows.

LIMIT: A rider who has not won six blue ribbons in one of these shows.

INTERMEDIATE: A rider who has not won twelve blue ribbons in one of these shows.

Since the only place where riders are judged rather than horses is in equitation classes, these terms of *maiden, novice,* etc., apply to junior riders. Ribbons won over fences raise your status in classes both over fences and on the flat. Ribbons won on the flat do not count toward your standing in classes over fences. You can be a limit rider on the flat and only a novice rider over fences, for example.

AMATEUR-OWNER: The owner of the horse or a member of his immediate family must ride in these classes. The amount of money or ribbons won by your horse is not considered in entry requirements.

THE HUNTER DIVISION

There are three groupings in this division: breeding (shown in hand), conformation (green and regular), and working (green and regular).

CONFORMATION: Conformation counts only a portion of the total points in any class in this division (except in model classes, where it counts one hundred percent). Usually conformation counts forty percent in conformation hunter classes. In the pony division, conformation counts only twenty-five percent. The judge will line up the class in the order of the ribbons after the performance section is finished. Then he will change the order on the basis of conformation.

I stood by the out gate at one A-rated show when one of the contestants of a conformation hunter class stood there watching the lineup. A beautiful chestnut with white socks was being moved up the line toward first place. He stopped short, however, in second place. The girl beside me gave a deep sigh. It was hard to know if she sighed in relief or anguish, because I didn't know which horse was hers. She had only said she had ridden a beautiful hunter round. When the blue ribbon was pinned on, then I knew. She beamed. Her handler came from the ring, and right behind him came her mother with a silver cup two feet high that the horse had won.

A conformation hunter must be a fine horse. Here, after a perfect round, the leading horse waits for the end of the conformation judging . . .

No wonder she had sighed when the other horse came so close to wiping out her lead.

MODEL CLASS: Conformation counts the total points. If you want the points won in this class to count toward a championship, you have to show over fences in the same show.

WORKING HUNTER: He is judged on performance; he must be sound, because that counts, too. Classes on the flat are called Hunter Under Saddle. You will find classes such as Green Hunter, or Regular Working Hunter (the height of the fences will be listed), or Regular Working Hunter Under Saddle (on the flat), or Junior Working Hunter (the rider under eighteen; the height of the fences lower than for an open class), or Working Hunter, Handy (a tricker course), or Amateur Owner Hunter Stake (the owner or someone from his family rides the horse over fences). Working Hunter is over fences unless it says "under saddle," or hack.

Some classes do not count toward a championship: Hunter Hack, Maiden, Novice, Limit, and Local hunter classes (those limited to horses stabled nearby).

HUNTER PONY: The AHSA sponsors a Hunter Pony competition. Ponies who win championship and reserve championship ribbons in Hunter Pony and Green Hunter Pony in an A-rated division qualify. Finals are judged

and wins.

A jumper need not be the most beautiful horse in the show, he only needs to jump. These two riders wait their turn for a junior-jumper class.

with performance on the flat, over fences, and conformation each counting a third.

JUNIOR HUNTER CLASSES: These classes are the same as those listed under the regular hunter division, only they are designed for junior riders. They are some of the largest classes in shows in many states, especially in the East. The fences are lower than for the regular hunter division. Some shows will have divisions by size, not only classes for large and small ponies but ones for different sizes of horses, too.

The judges consider manners and also the suitability of the pony or horse for his rider. Your mount should "fit" you. Once you have outgrown a pony, it is hard to compete in pony classes because you look too big.

These are not equitation classes, even though the riders are juniors. The pony or horse is judged on his ability, way of going, and how he takes fences.

THE JUMPER DIVISION

Classes are judged on how well your horse jumps. Jumper classes are run according to Tables set up by the AHSA. Each Table has specific rules that determine how the class is run. In some classes (Table I) touches count so that these are often called "Touch Classes." In others (Table II and III) time counts, so that the riders are said to be jumping "against the clock."

PRELIMINARY JUMPER: In the three classifications for jumpers, preliminary is the lowest. Horses entered here have won less than one thousand dollars in a specified period of time. Fences are lower than in the other sections.

INTERMEDIATE JUMPER: Horses who have won one thousand dollars but not yet earned three thousand dollars. Your horse is considered an intermediate jumper if he has been entered in any International Combined Training Event. Once your horse qualifies as an intermediate jumper he cannot go back to compete in preliminary, although he can enter open jumper classes.

OPEN JUMPER: A horse who has won over three thousand dollars. You may enter open jumper classes if you have won less money, but you cannot go back to easier classes once you qualify as an open jumper. You are allowed to drop back a division if your horse hasn't shown for a year or won less than one thousand dollars the last year he showed. The courses are more difficult, the fences wider and higher in the open classes.

JUNIOR JUMPER CLASSES: A junior rider (one under eighteen) rides the courses. Classes are judged the same as in the jumping division. Your horse or pony must have good manners.

EQUITATION

These classes are judged on seat and hands. The riders are juniors. Some classes are held on the flat, some over fences.

MEDAL CLASS: These classes are sponsored by the AHSA, of which you must be a member in order to enter. One of the four medal classes is the AHSA Hunter Seat Medal Class. You must be under eighteen to be eligible. Qualification for the finals is based on the blue ribbons you win. You need three from the large riding states (such as Connecticut, New York, New Jersey, or Pennsylvania). If you live in some other states you need two blue ribbons and in many you only need one. Everyone who qualifies is given a Silver Medal—an honor that means an exceptionally fine rider. The final rideoffs are held at large shows in the fall.

THE ORGANIZATION BEHIND SHOWS

RECOGNIZED SHOW: A show run by a member of the American Horse Show Association. There are different types of recognized shows. They include Local Shows and Regular Member Shows, as well as ones for Combined Training, Dressage, etc.

REGULAR MEMBER SHOWS: These shows have different ratings. A-rated shows are the most difficult of all shows. You will often have international competition. Top riders from your state and across the country are drawn to A shows. Points for classes are higher. More classes are held and the prize money is higher than for other types of shows. The show lasts several days. A show can be rated A in one division and C in another, and the prize money and points are specified by the classification. The names of winners are forwarded by the show management to the AHSA.

A B show has fewer classes and lower prize money than an A show, but the points awarded winners are still double those for a C show—the lowest category.

HORSE OF THE YEAR AWARD: The horse who wins the most points in each division of a Regular Member Show of the American Horse Shows Association. Championships carry the most points at competing shows, Reserve Championship the next most, and on through fourth-place ribbons. Your horse must be registered with the AHSA to be eligible for the award.

THE RULE BOOK: The American Horse Shows Association sends out its rule book to all its members each year. (You cannot get a copy without becoming a member.) You need a current copy if you show.

I asked my friend Leslie, who had my rule book open on her table, what she had learned from reading it. "Lots," she said. "I found out that I couldn't use bell boots on my hunter in the show, and I was planning to, and that you can't dye your horse."

The rule book not only answers all your questions in clear language, but it gives some helpful hints on riding. Don't skip the sections for show committees, for example, just because you aren't on one. The explanations on how to design courses are great for those who plan to ride them.

WHERE DO YOU START?

YOUR FIRST SHOW: Begin with unrecognized and local shows because the competition is less stiff. If you have an exceptional horse, these shows will not affect his status while you are learning. You can find out where shows are to be held by watching your local newspaper, subscribing to *The Chronicle of the Horse,* asking at the nearby saddlery, checking at stables, obtaining a rule book of the AHSA, which lists all its members' shows.

Young riders will find the most pleasant way to learn about the show world is to become members of a local Pony Club or the 4-H Club.

WHICH CLASSES FIRST?: Classes on the flat include pleasure horse, hack, some equitation classes, and under saddle classes.

Maiden classes are the easiest because those who enter have not won a blue ribbon. If you are young, your age is an advantage because some classes are limited to riders under eleven, or fourteen, or eighteen.

If you want to jump, look at the class requirements where the height of the course is specified. Pony classes are designed for young riders and are good ones for starters.

I listened to Martha Maynard discussing with her instructor which classes she could enter with her young mare. The show coming up was B rated, but it was the first for her horse. "I'd try local hunter," her instructor said, "which limits the entries to horses from fifty miles around. Not that that does you too much good, since some of the best riding establishments in the country are within fifty miles of here. But it will cut down some."

"Can't I go in green hunter?" she asked.

He debated a moment, then decided she could. The horse had the ability, and he knew she could ride well.

A similar debate between rider and instructor took place at Ox Ridge Hunt Club. This girl had ridden in more shows and had an experienced horse. "Did you enter the Medals and Maclay?" the instructor asked.

"Everything except the USET," the girl said. "I wasn't sure about intermediate hunter. I've won about a dozen ribbons. After counting carefully, the girl decided she only had eleven blue ribbons. So she entered both intermediate and open classes. One more ribbon would have put her beyond the intermediate level.

The jargon of the show world is not so difficult to learn. After you have ridden in a show or two, it all comes clear. You can learn it by watching shows, too, if you pay attention and aren't afraid to ask questions.

8
Clothes and Tack

CLOTHES HELP THE RIDER

"Someone must have a jacket I can borrow," Janet moaned the night before her first show. Although she rode at a riding camp, she had never anticipated being good enough to ride in an "outside" show. She had been chosen as a replacement at the last minute out of the seventy-five campers in her division.

"I'm going to ride in a 'real show' tomorrow. *Me!*" She rummaged through her trunk and came up with a white blouse that almost looked ironed.

While Janet worried, the riding director scurried from tent to tent trying to find someone with a jacket that not only would fit Janet but would look right on her. She turned down a scarlet one. Though Janet didn't know it, the riding director looked just as hard for a blouse and choker. She wasn't out to have her riders only enter the show, she wanted them dressed to win. By midnight she wore a smile. She finally had rounded up enough breeches, boots, jackets, and hats to outfit all eight girls who were riding.

Her work paid off. Janet and her friends came home with six ribbons among them. Dress alone did not win the ribbons, but without it the girls might not have been in the running so often.

When you go to a riding store to buy an outfit, keep your horse in mind. Not only must your clothes go well with your coloring and the kind of rider you are, they should go well with your horse. Be conservative. Choose the subdued colors. Avoid canary breeches and a black coat because they are the sign of an amateur. This does not mean you cannot buy a black coat if black is your color and makes your horse look smart. Try to

Conservative dress that goes well with the rider and complements the horse. Tailored shirt and tie are correct for men.

know something about fashion and style. Then you'll feel better in the show ring.

Neatness is the key when you dress for a show. Clean clothes, pressed clothes, clothes that fit, mark the careful dresser. Your hair should be caught into a net or tucked into your hat. Once, when I watched a horse show with a woman who had been training riders for shows for half a century, she gave a disgusted grunt at a rider going by. She looked excellent on her horse, but each time she posted her hair flopped on her shoulders. "Doesn't

A beautifully turned-out rider wears a properly fitted, pressed jacket, neat choker and pin, polished boots, preferably handmade, and nicely fitting breeches. A choker and pin are better than a tie. Wear no jewelry—not even earrings in pierced ears. Boots should be black hunt boots or brown field boots. Boots that are high and fit snugly give a slim look to your leg.

A hair net is a must to hold all flying ends for girls. Men, too, must keep long hair back and neat, or in a pony tail as here.

that look terrible," my friend said. The judge must have agreed—no ribbon. The show ring just isn't the place for soft, floating hair—a man's or a woman's—tuck it up.

TACK FOR YOUR HORSE

Your tack is your horse's clothes. Choose it with the same care as you do your own outfit. You'll need a hunter saddle that fits you—something you can test in the riding store—but buy one that also fits your horse. A hunter saddle makes a better impression on a judge than a flat saddle does. You should use a hunter saddle even in classes on the flat. Sometimes you will see Arabs or Morgans in road hack, pleasure horse, or equitation classes without hunter saddles—and they often do well. But these are exceptions.

Never use new tack in a show. If you are one of the fortunate ones who can afford two sets of tack, a set for shows is a pure delight. Once you have your saddle, take good care of it. The keepers, the stirrup leathers, the skirts, every part of it should have the supple feel of much saddle-soaping. Even the stirrups should be polished. Your saddle must be in perfect condition, too.

The bridle should fit correctly. Like your saddle, keep it saddle-soaped,

Gloves are a good touch to your outfit.

Spurs for the rider who knows how to use them. They are optional in equitation classes. Do not wear them in hunter under saddle.

soft, intact. Leslie spent eighty-five dollars for a new bridle for Decision one fall. She felt so proud of it. The snaffle worked well on him; she did well in shows. Then winter came. Bounce went Decision. If the snaffle alone wouldn't hold him, what could she do? In desperation she called the horse's former owner. *She* had used a dropped noseband. This meant one more expense. Happily for Leslie, it worked. But she would have been more pleased if she had bought it in the first place.

There might have been other solutions to her problem. Sometimes a rider can get along without a snaffle in a show. Sometimes he is required to use a double bridle or pelham for a particular class. If, like Leslie, you have a new part to your bridle, or an entirely new bridle for a show, darken it with oil to make it looked used.

Not only must the rider have the immaculate look, his horse should look special, too. The unusual markings of this horse set off the hunter saddle (which is the type to use) and the snaffle bit (the most acceptable bridle for hunters). In some classes judges may require pelhams or double bridles.

Polish your stirrups. The saddle pad must fit. It must be clean or new. A martingale may not be used in classes on the flat. You may use one in classes that combine work on the flat and over fences: AHSA, ASPCA, and USET classes. It is permitted in jumping classes.

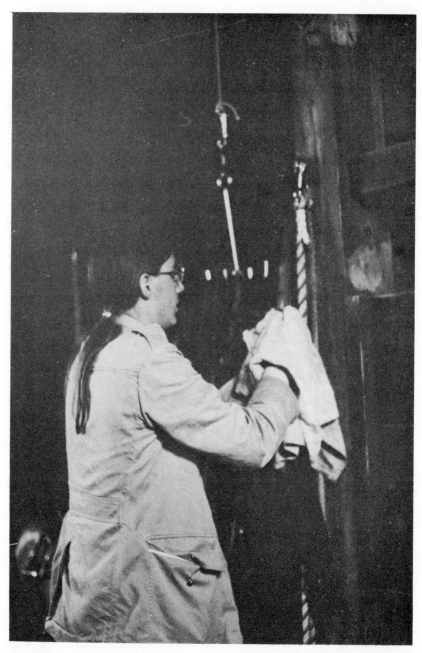

"Water won't hurt your girth if you hone it off right away. Some children just don't think about caked mud hurting a horse," Tibby Hunt said as she worked on a girth at a muddy show. So keep your tack clean even after you arrive.

The pad you use can be a real asset in the ring. At one show a chestnut horse with a red saddle pad bordered in white made a striking appearance. The bright new pad made the horse quickly noted. A pad that contrasts with your horse's color is always good. A white pad (which is imitation sheepskin) looks well on a black horse or one that is dark in color. Most horses look well with sheepskin pads. If you cannot come up with a new pad, or one that looks new, you can go without. This is hard on your saddle, however. It is better to go without than to ride with a pad that fits poorly.

Rob had a saddle that fit him well and made him feel secure whenever he rode. Before his first show, he bought a new sheepskin pad. In spite of his delight in his saddle, he thought of the expense of the pad and didn't have the courage to cut it to fit the saddle in case he wanted another saddle later. So he trotted off to the show with his new pad sticking up all around, feeling proud and looking foolish.

A martingale can be a problem at a horse show. Usually the rules for a class tell you if a martingale is allowed. You cannot wear a martingale in hack, under saddle or tie-breaking classes.

You want to conform when you ride. The way you dress, the way your horse looks, are conventions that have grown up through the years. Horse shows preserve these traditions. You can almost imagine an ideal—what makes the perfect horse and perfect rider—and then conform to it in every detail. This is what puts you in the ribbons. Individual initiative and ingenuity are seldom rewarded. The trained horse and rider, the disciplined look, will beat out the individualist every time—or almost every time.

Once, not so long ago, at a horse show in Greenwich, Connecticut, a tall young girl on a tall chestnut horse entered a class with thirty other horses. She had the look of confidence written all over her. And she wore a bright green riding jacket. She stood out from every other rider in the ring, but she could afford to stand out. The judge asked for a program ride, nothing else. The green-coated rider managed to head the line. She rode a flawless performance. No one, not even the judge (though he marked his card for the other places), needed to see anyone else. The blue ribbon was hers before her horse slid to a stop at the exact spot, to the inch, that the judge had indicated—which proves, perhaps, that if you can ride better than any other rider in the show, you can wear green or purple or anything else you please.

9

Getting Your Horse Ready for the Show

CLIPPING

Your horse, like you, must be neat. He can't use a hair net for long stray hairs, so you clip him. All over. If he has a hunter clip, his legs may have longer hair in the winter as a protection in the field.

Remember to clip his whiskers, his fetlocks, his ears (even in the summer), if you are going to show.

TAIL

If your horse has a long tail, you should pull it until it is about halfway up his cannon bone. You are also permitted to cut it straight across, but pulling makes a nicer looking job.

A bushy tail also has to be pulled. Don't pull hairs from behind. You need those for braiding. Pull them from the sides to make his tail look narrow and slim. For local shows you may not need to braid the tail at all, as long as it is pulled and clean.

Always shampoo the mane and tail the day before the show and rinse them out completely. Wash his white markings at the same time.

You can braid your horse the night before the show if you are very slow at it. Wrap his tail in a bandage to protect it and keep him from rubbing ends loose. However, it is best to braid both mane and tail the day of the show, because you will get a neater effect with fewer broken hairs and pricky ends. If the tail is to be braided again, you cannot braid the night before since it breaks too many hairs—and you don't want to run out of

Your horse must be spotlessly groomed. A pulled mane is acceptable in small shows, but even there braids make a better impression. In the jumper division, anything goes.

them. Braids *do* help him look neat. Not that big show riders *always* braid. Even in the National Horse Show in Madison Square Garden one or two hunter entries dared flout the custom. But if you make the Garden, and if your horse's mane has a flaxen, flowing, groomed-forever look, you might be able to forget the braids, too. Jumpers, of course, are usually shown without braids.*

SHOES

Check your horse's shoes and have him reshod a week before the show

---

* An illustrated explanation of clipping and braiding can be found in *Grooming Your Horse* by the author.

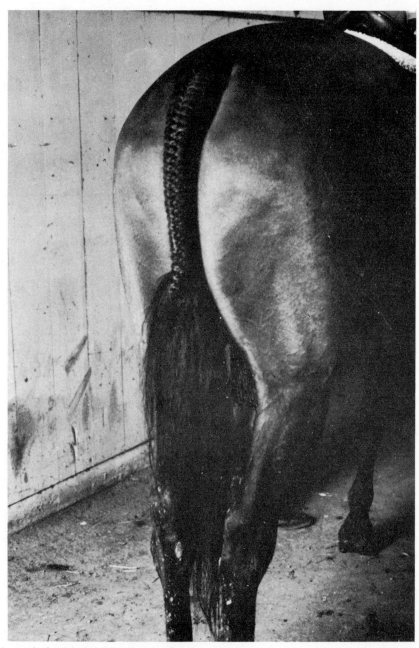

A neatly braided tail is a work of art.

Braids are part of showing. The neat, sleek look they give a horse make his whole appearance finer. Don't let prickly ends show. Make tight braids that are folded under twice and sewn with thread the color of his mane.

if you possibly can. Always check his shoes before he goes into a class. Oddly enough, you are permitted to continue if your horse throws a shoe during a class—but the decision is up to you.

Scrub his hoofs the day before the show and oil them thoroughly. It's a good idea to bring hoof dressing to the show and give a last minute wipe over his hoofs before he goes into the ring.

TAKE ALONG

His own pails. Grain and hay, and possibly his own water. Rags for rubbing him down. Old towels are great. Hoof dressing. A couple pairs of bell boots and an extra pair of riding gloves in case of rain. A lead shank. A sponge for wiping his eyes and nose before a class. A sheet or blanket. And a snack for you. Although shows usually have refreshment booths, sometimes you are in a hurry, or the lines are long.

ARRIVING AT THE SHOW

If you hack to the show, allow an hour more than you think it will take you. Somehow, no matter how carefully you plan, it takes longer to get ready and get there than you expect. For a one-day show, plan to arrive at least an hour ahead of the starting time. A longer show gives you the chance to come early, to look over the courses, and to let your horse get used to this strange place.

Try to find an out-of-the-way spot for parking. Your horse will like that. If the parking area is crowded, choose a location where there will be as little traffic past your van as possible. You don't want your horse bumped by a passing fender, or upset by a constant stream of people, horses, and cars barging past him.

It's hard not to feel superior to the crowd—after all, they have come to watch *you*. Remember, though, people also have to get around from place to place, and if the show is outdoors, from ring to ring. The paths do not belong exclusively to horses. Spectators should be treated courteously, even when they do stupid things and run in front of you at the worst moment. In a way, a horse show is a performance before an audience. They pay to see it. So be good to them.

When you arrive at your first show, you are more interested in training your horse to accept the wild happenings around him than in anything else. He has to adjust to the loudspeaker, the waving programs, music, and more horses and people than he has seen in one place before. It's scary. Let him walk around and absorb it all. Don't go galloping up and down to greet

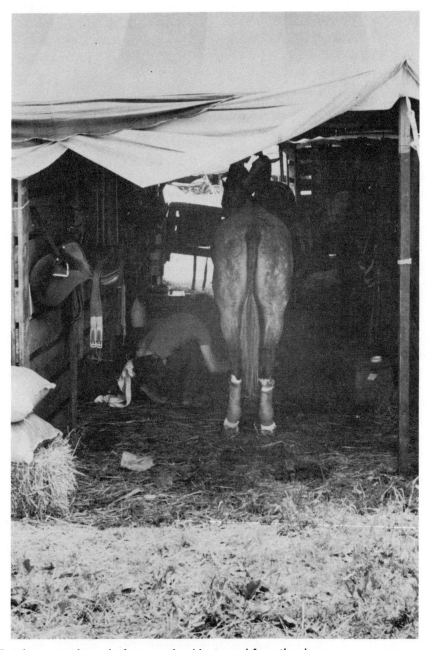

Bandage your horse before vanning him to and from the show.

Come prepared for mud. Four out of five days at this show it rained.

friends, or rush over a schooling fence. Your quiet attitude is the best way to make him take the whole thing in his stride.

Your horse will have to be quiet under unusual circumstances at some shows. One day, at a big show, someone suddenly decided to turn on the music on the loud speaker, right in the middle of a hunter class. A young girl's horse was just coming off a fence when the music blared behind her. It was so loud the whole audience swung around, and many covered their ears. What about the horse? He kept right on cantering into the next set of fences, a combination, and never missed a stride or a fence. That is show presence.

Try not to be self-centered. Don't be afraid to smile and say the first "hello." Watch how others work out their horses; you may learn a trick or

You can see the checkerboarding (the design) done so neatly on the croup. It is done with a stencil or small comb. First wet the hair, then brush or comb it in the opposite direction.

two. When you have an opportunity to watch classes, don't just sit there reveling in being there—a part of it all—see what you can learn by examining how other riders use their hands, how they take turns, how they correct faults. You have a chance to see experts at work.

PART III

Showing

10

Pleasure Horse and Hack Classes

Either of these classes are good ones to begin with in your first show. They will be large, but you will be able to do everything the judge asks. Classes on the flat, such as these, have no fences—no jumps. Judges look at the young riders in one of these classes, recognize their inexperience, and take it into account in their judging. Sometimes you find older adults in pleasure horse classes, men and women who have fine horses, have shown in the past and enjoy it, but no longer want to risk taking fences.

WHAT ARE YOU ASKED TO DO?

You will be given a few minutes to warm up after you enter the ring. Don't wear out your horse, but you can practice whatever gait you like: walk, trot, canter. Be sure, by the time the class begins, that you have your horse off by himself, not in the middle of the bunch.

Walk comes first. Find a hole for yourself if you haven't before, either by circling, or crossing the ring. Don't cut off the judge's view as you do it. Almost immediately you will be asked to trot.

Again you will walk, but only a short distance, perhaps only a fourth of the way around the ring. Get ready—canter comes next. Prepare to take the correct lead; keep your horse awake. Although a judge likes a horse who takes his canter right away, he likes better the one who takes the correct lead, even if it takes a bit longer.

Reverse now. Then walk, trot, and canter going in the new direction.

Line up. Be sure your horse doesn't barge in among the other horses. Manners show here. Sometimes, not always, you are asked to back.

A pleasure horse should go with a loose rein. He should carry his head forward. You will be asked to trot and canter both directions of the ring.

You may be asked to take the rail in a large class. The judge may need a second look to pick one place, or he may be breaking a tie. He may already have his first-place winner and leave him standing in the center. You never know for sure. So whether you are on the rail riding your best or standing in the center waiting—keep your show look.

WHAT HELPS YOU WIN?

Attitude. A true showman has the look of a horseman and knows it. He pays attention to what he is doing every moment. No winks at friends along the fence. He is ever conscious of what other horses are doing so that he never gets boxed. Somehow he avoids trouble before it starts. Every moment he acts as if he knows the judge is judging him.

Placement helps. When you enter the ring, come in by yourself rather than with the crowd. That's likely to be first time the judge notices you, so give him a good chance to make the most of it. The more you can stay where he can see you, the better chance you have to win. No matter how good you are, if the judge doesn't get to see you, he can't pin you. So stay in the open; don't always let another horse get on your inside, cutting you off from the judge. If the class is large, you must find a time when your horse is going exceptionally well and make sure the judge sees him. However, no judge likes a horse who interferes with his vision by constantly getting between him and the class. Rushing around the center won't win any points. It is good to ride on the rail, especially if you get an open spot there. Listen carefully to instructions, but don't turn around to watch the judge.

Move along smartly. Keep the gait asked without breaking. At a walk, you want long, ground-covering strides. At a trot, your horse should move alertly, seem to enjoy his work, yet look relaxed. Don't whiz past everyone on the inside, nor lag either. At a canter, check your lead. Watch it especially if asked to take a canter from a trot, something more and more judges ask to see. Many judges like a canter so slow that it appears to be slow-motion, but is still graceful. Only take a rocking-chair canter if your horse is exceptional doing it. You cannot risk fumbling or breaking gait. He should back immediately when you ask, three or four steps in succession on diagonal legs in a straight line. Watch the judge for your cue. When he walks behind you, move back as alertly as you would move forward.

Your horse's attitude is important. He should be responsive. When you ask for a walk after a canter, he should come back to it quickly and willingly without a hard tug, without tucking his head to his chest, without opening his mouth. He should look as if he enjoys every moment. Pricked ears are great assets. If your horse always looks sour, don't make it worse by jerking his mouth or kicking him by mistake. Manners count. Good manners may not win for you, but bad manners can lose.

Control is vital. A hand gallop means a gallop "in hand," not a race. Often eight horses are kept in the ring to gallop together. You will be given a moment to walk along the rail after the rest of the class is dismissed, then comes the gallop. Don't outgallop the whole field! When you are asked to halt, stop then and there or you are out. This willing, pliable obedience is proof of control and manners both. A nose pointing to the stars is a sure sign of resistance.

Quietness is another good quality, both in you and your horse. Stand at attention when you line up. Make your horse stand straight so that one leg isn't crooked. But do it without fussing and fidgeting or trying many times. Then keep him standing quietly while you sit quietly. Don't talk to the rider beside you. Don't laugh or giggle.

Mistakes happen. You seldom ride as well in a show as you do at home, but don't get flustered about it. If something goes wrong, correct it calmly and go on.

Of course, you can never quite tell the kind of impression your horse will make on the judge. This can be good, or it can be bad; it depends on the horse. Saucy Melody always had her ears forward. She was the picture of perkiness in any show ring. Often she fooled the judge. But her rider knew better and secretly had her fingers crossed the whole time. Her rider knew the farther forward Saucy Melody had her ears, the more likely she was to do something. In fact, you could be sitting on her back, beating and kicking her, and her ears would be forward! So anything could happen at any time in the ring.

PLEASURE HORSE CLASS

The quiet, easy and free moving horse wins. This kind of horse is a pleasure to ride. The ideal pleasure horse goes on a loose rein at every gait. A snaffle is the choice bit, because a snaffle appears to prove your horse is

You want a relaxed horse in pleasure horse classes, but one that also moves well.

easy to handle. Some judges, however, require a pelham bit. A horse who does anything at the drop of a hat is certainly the type you'd choose for a pleasurable ride, and so would the judge. These classes are likely to be the largest in the horse show because everyone thinks his horse is pleasurable.

Any breed of horse can be entered in a pleasure-horse class. Pretty horses are better liked, of course, but they need not be Thoroughbreds. Pricked ears are a sign of pleasantness; an easy alert trot proof of an enjoyable ride. Your horse should move from the shoulder rather than the knee.

You will be asked to back, but not to take a hand gallop. The usual routine for classes on the flat will be followed.

Your ability to make your horse look good in the ring is all that matters. Outside the ring, the same horse may be terrible, but the judge isn't judging outside the ring. Sassy, a most stubborn mule at times, gave her owners some breath-holding moments whenever she entered a pleasure horse class. Sassy *appeared* to be the perfect pleasure horse. Chestnut in color, dainty in build, a registered Saddlebred to give her the look of breeding, and even that gentle, slow-motion canter marked her as a blue-ribbon winner. Judges, watching her, agreed—when she behaved.

Both horse and rider should turn out a relaxed picture.

Sassy's favorite stunt was to stop dead in the middle of a canter. If her rider hit her with the crop, Sassy would lay back her ears, buck, balk for several seconds, and then canter sweetly again. She might look like a pushbutton horse, but she hated to extend at a trot or canter; in fact, she hated to move out at all.

She had another act: she'd kick out at other horses when they were cantering. All the time they were going around together, Sassy would look the part of an angel. But everyone who knew her would see the look in her eye that she was just waiting—waiting for a second until she could get that horse. Her rider had to keep a crop in readiness, prepared to show it to Sassy, prepared to use it just right behind the saddle.

The judge would always call back ten horses or so in the big classes Sassy entered. Not once was she omitted from the elite group. At one show there were at least thirty horses in the class and only six ribbons. In the midst of one canter, Sassy stopped dead. She gave one of the longest bucks her owners had ever seen, then almost backed up, but finally was brought into a canter again. By some freak the judge didn't see her! Here, in a class of all these perfectly mannered horses, Sassy came in sixth.

The command class is one of the favorites in Buffalo, New York, shows. Any horse who fails to obey a command instantly is out. Now Sassy is a pretty horse, nicely put together, and she is well trained. You just couldn't tell when she might get nasty. In this particular command class there were forty horses, split into two groups. She was in the running for the ribbons, doing perfectly. After ten minutes of hard work, she still performed with top quality. The judge didn't know how many who knew her had clenched fists and faces puffed red from holding their breath as they watched from the sidelines. Then he asked for a canter from a stop. Sassy swished her tail, laid back her ears, tossed her head, gave a buck and refused to budge for three or four seconds. That was the end of her in that class. *She* had simply decided she had had enough.

HACK CLASSES

These classes are similar to pleasure horse classes. The idea behind the class is to choose a horse who is good for hacking along on road and trails. It should be one who moves along nicely without tiring. Usually this means a long stride.

But not always. In one road hack class a girl entered who had had her pony a long time. She had raised and trained him herself, and loved him dearly. There wasn't anything he wouldn't try to do for her. He wasn't pretty, which is one reason she entered the road hack class—he might have a chance. No one paid any attention to him until he trotted. Then the

In the road hack class, your horse should have a ground-covering stride. You must do an extended trot. Ideally, his foreleg moves forward in a line from his shoulder. This horse has good engagment of his haunches and freedom of shoulder.

crowd sat up and took notice. Never had a pony gone so fast. His little legs whizzed along, covering ground as if he barely touched it. He just tore up the turf on his extended trot. In fact, he looked comical. No one, however, was prepared for him to win a ribbon. He didn't place high, but he placed. The announcer said, "And in fifth place we have the fastest pony on earth . . .," which broke up the crowd. And thrilled the pony's owner.

Your horse needs to have one of the pony's qualities—the ability to cover ground quickly and easily. A judge likes him to have other qualities, too. He ought to be responsive and happy about his work.

You are expected to ride with loose reins as you do in a pleasure horse class. A snaffle is not always the best bridle, although some judges prefer it here as well. Sometimes double reins are specified, and there are judges who like to see double bridles. Don't try to put a double bridle on your horse just for the show. It takes getting used to. If your horse has a real dislike for two bits, try a pelham instead. If you have to have a double bridle, the rules will say so. Smaller shows are less strict, but it is a good idea to check it out before you get into the show ring.

A judge is not going to like a horse who sticks his head high, unless he carries it high naturally. An arched neck does not give the relaxed look, either, but a horse who carries his head collected and well in balance looks soft and easy. Some classes will have saddle horses as well as hunters in them, and the judge will not expect the saddle horses to go on a loose rein.

WAYS ROAD HACK DIFFERS FROM PLEASURE HORSE

You will need to know three speeds of the trot for the road-hack class. When the judge asks for the extended trot, he wants an extended trot, one in which the horse really throws his legs out and covers a lot of ground with each stride. A horse who really extends more than at a fast trot is going to be noticed. If he appears to be floating over the ground without effort he is going to be among those who are called back. The judge is not likely to ask for a sitting trot in the road hack class!

A hand gallop is expected. Don't start passing everything in the ring; don't go rocking along either. Gallop under control. The more brilliant horse will be pinned higher in road hack than in pleasure horse.

You may come across hunter hack classes in which two simple jumps are required. They will be low, however, and shouldn't cause most horses any trouble at all. If you are determined not to go over any fences, check the specifications before you register for the class. A hack class can be held to judge top riders if it is used to break a tie in a hunter division. Then it means the riders "hack off"—no fences—and the best rider on the flat wins.

11

Equitation—Hunt Seat

Equitation classes are for young riders. Officially, under AHSA rules, they are for juniors. However, shows are now offering equitation classes for adults, too. Remember, in equitation, the rider, not the horse is being judged. Shows offer maiden classes (the rider hasn't won a single blue ribbon), novice (he hasn't won three blues), limit (he hasn't won six blues), intermediate (he hasn't won twelve blues), and open classes. There are classes on the flat as well as ones over fences.

HOW ARE YOU JUDGED?

Your riding form, your hands, the way you handle your horse, all enter into the judging. "I watch the decisions riders make and how they execute them," Tibby Hunt said of judging equitation classes.

You must sit erect, commanding, yet relaxed. Your legs must be motionless. The movement of your hands is identical with the movement of the bit, which makes them appear very quiet. A deep seat is essential. If you have that special look, that indefinable something a few riders are born with, you could be in the ribbons. A pleasant, proficient attitude, a business-like approach to your task can take the place of natural aptitude. Keep your attention focused on your horse, your ears and the back of your mind conscious of the judge, and a part of you sensitive to the movement of other horses so that you stay clear of the crowd.

EQUITATION ON THE FLAT

You will walk, trot and canter in both directions. The judge might ask for a canter from either a walk or a trot, so watch your leads. Be sure to use your hands and legs both when you back. Three speeds of the trot are part of many classes. A sitting trot tests your balance. Post to an ordinary trot. You may either sit or post to an extended trot. The real test of a secure seat and balance comes if you are asked to ride without stirrups. Mounting and dismounting should appear easy. (Don't forget to check the girth before you remount. It may be unnecessary but it should be routine.)

MAIDEN EQUITATION

A judge knows you are just beginning to show. He won't be rough on you. He even takes into account that you aren't wearing the best riding outfit money can buy. "Just be sure it fits, even if your mother has to take it in for you," Tibby Hunt says.

Once, when I was judging a camp show, a teenager came to me shyly and asked, "Do you count off if someone doesn't have a riding outfit?" I knew half the campers didn't have them and told her it didn't matter. When this girl's class entered the ring, she alone had no jacket. Any judge is able to look beneath the clothes to see the rider's skill, but riding clothes make the task easier because they are neat and don't cover up a rider's motion with bags and bulges. The girl came in fifth. I felt my explanation of why fell flat. Perhaps she sensed that clothes help. Perhaps she just needed the confidence they would have given her.

Maiden riders sometimes forget diagonals, and in their excitement even goof on leads. You *can* have show presence; you can remember everything. But, if you make a mistake, don't panic. Go ahead. Everyone else may make mistakes, too.

NOVICE EQUITATION

The judge expects more of you here. You have had some show experience, which makes you more relaxed. The time you may find this class difficult is in a show when no maiden class is offered and you are forced into novice.

You can be asked for a hand gallop, to trot a figure eight (watch your diagonals), and to canter a figure eight with a simple change of lead (coming back to a trot or walk before cantering the second loop).

LIMIT AND INTERMEDIATE EQUITATION

More flexibility, more responsiveness, and a higher degree of skill mark the limit rider. He has ridden in many shows to reach this status, because blue ribbons do not come easily. This is even more true of an intermediate rider. The judge will ask for more difficult tests in these classes.

EQUITATION OVER FENCES

This is the place where you have to prove you can control your horse, take jumps smoothly, and show perfect form. In the thousands of photographs I have taken of children and young people jumping, barely a one is without faults in position. A perfect jump is ever so hard to make. It takes practice and practice and practice. This is one reason why you spend so much time over low fences. A judge assumes you would not enter an equitation class over fences unless your horse could jump. So if he knocks down a fence, it is going to count off.

The procedure for all hunter and equitation over fences classes is the same. Enter the ring with the alert look and heads-up confidence you want the judge to see. Make a circle that uses about a fourth of the ring. Any gait is permitted, but it is a good idea to start with a trot or walk, then halfway round break into a canter. Take the lead you want for the first set of fences. Make a straight approach to the first one.

At one show, I was taking pictures so I couldn't notice entire rounds. One girl stood out just the same. I noticed her. She made jumping look easy. You'd think it was nothing at all to go over all those fences. She won the blue ribbon.

The most *applause* went to a small boy. Near the end of the course, his horse ran out on a fence. With a mighty tug, the boy pulled him back, got him to circle and come at the fence again. Over it they went, but the horse barged past the next one. Once more he hauled him around, turned him to the fence, and then gave a yell that resounded from the roof. His exasperation showed in that yell. Whether his horse finished the course beautifully because of the yell or because the yell meant determination, who can tell? No ribbons were awarded his rider that day, but in a couple of years, the story will be different. A pushbutton horse, a neat ride, may win for you today, but the determination and courage it takes to train a horse well are what will keep you winning. Equitation is judged not just on how you look but on how you ride, as well.

A pony is sometimes the best mount you can have. Ponies do well over the low fences of maiden and novice classes. If you are a small rider, do not scorn a pony as a show entry. They make good starting mounts.

Maiden classes will have low fences and a simple course. You might have as few as six fences. Often there are four and you make two rounds. Your horse would stay on the same lead all the way around in that case. A beginning position for your hands (resting on the crest) as you go over the jumps is permitted.

In a novice class the judge will expect better form and more assurance.

You should show you know how to put a horse into a fence. This means you are less a passenger and more of a guiding hand.

The courses in a limit class will be more difficult. A figure-eight course is not unusual. Turns are sharper, and you will have changes of lead. It is nice if your horse makes flying changes because this gives you a smoother round. Always give your horse as much room as you can coming into a fence. Take wide curves when there is room for them. The hunter pace, moving quickly but under control, gives the smoothest effect.

OPEN EQUITATION

The competition is stiff because the riders have won many times in other equitation classes. Consider the rating of the show, too. An A show is tougher than a B one. In fact, riders who are accustomed to riding in A shows usually get pinned if they drop down to a B show. The horses and riders in an A-rated show are often so good that a dozen or more could get the blue ribbon and deserve it. But a judge is there to make a decision on how well you ride *that* day. The breaks of the game come into play. Your horse may have a brilliant round and you are in. But if he feels sour, you are out. You may have shown in many classes and it is hard to be at your best all the time. Little things enter into winning in a class where every competitor is tops.

Open equitation classes on the flat can demand a dozen tests of the rider. These could include a figure eight at a canter with a flying change of lead, or cantering down the center of the ring making simple changes of lead, or performing at every gait without stirrups. You could be asked to pick up an inside lead, interrupt your canter and take an outside lead, interrupt again and take the inside lead again. Part of the time you would be doing a countercanter. One of the most difficult tests is changing horses. It counts double. Judges prefer not to change horses just because it is time consuming, but sometimes it is the only way to be sure of a rider's ability. A rider, familiar with his horse's quirks of character, or his odd gait, can ride so that the problem has no effect on him. Another rider on his horse is less fortunate. This is one reason why you should watch other riders at a show. You discover how they manage difficult situations. It can pay big dividends. The best practice you can get is to ride different horses frequently.

At a riding camp one of the girls fell so in love with Inkspot that she wouldn't ride anything else. He was difficult to ride, mainly because he broke into a trot unless his rider knew how to keep him calm. During a show, this girl had to change horses. Everything she had learned on Inkspot was wrong for the other mount. She looked terrible on him. The other rider must have known horses similar to Inkspot for she cockily handled him just right and rode off with the blue ribbon.

A strong canter: it is between an ordinary and extended canter. This schooling movement is used to teach the horse lateral flexion. It is achieved by softening the hand and using the leg to push the horse forward to meet the bit. Your seat stays in the saddle.

Open equitation classes over fences can bring you up against Medal and Maclay riders and even those who are competing in United States Equestrian Team classes. All these classes are held at the same show, so expect a tough class. Of course, at smaller shows you will meet fewer of the top-notch riders. In some parts of the country the competition is easier, but don't count on it.

The fences in open equitation will be higher and trickier. An in and out, a combination, changes of direction are standard. The course itself will be more complex. Be ready to ride it without stirrups—it can happen.

TOP EQUITATION CLASSES: MEDAL, MACLAY, USET

Medal classes, in which you must win one or more blue ribbons to

Turn on the forehand: keep a feel of the reins to prevent him from stepping forward; use slight pressure on the right rein as you press your right leg behind the girth; keep your left leg at the girth so he won't step backward. His right hind leg should cross in front of his left hind leg. Reverse the aids for a left turn on the forehand.

Turn on the haunches: lead the forehand around with the right rein, but with support from the left; your left leg presses behind the girth to prevent a shift of his hindquarters; your right leg at the girth gets impulsion and keeps him from stepping backward. His left foreleg should cross in front of his right foreleg. His right hind foot marks time in the same spot. For a left turn on the haunches, reverse your aids. (Be careful your reins do not get a bit long as here, and his head should bend with his movement.)

The countercanter: his leading foreleg (his left) is on the *outside* of his circle (toward the fence).

compete in the finals, give you tough competition. They will be judged both by your performance over fences and on the flat. At a recent A-rated show, there were only thirty riders in this class, yet the judge called back six of them to repeat just half the course and do two simple additional things: pull up in front of a fence and back. That was all he needed to see to choose his winners. The usual procedure for a medals class is to call back the top four to six riders. They are asked to work off tests one to seventeen either on the flat or over fences.

Maclay classes, those sponsored by The American Society of Prevention of Cruelty to Animals (called Maclay after the donor of the trophy), are equally difficult. Judges in different parts of the country vary the order and what they ask. Usually, however, the whole class competes over a course, which counts fifty percent. Then the judge calls back the top twelve riders (if there are that many he can choose). These work off on the flat, which counts the other fifty percent. From this group he picks his winners. The classes, too, are more difficult where the competition is stiffer, where more riders have excellent trainers, and where there are simply a lot more horses competing in shows.

The United States Equestrian Team classes were set up to encourage riders to emulate the top nonprofessional riders in the country who are members of the United States Equestrian Team, to increase interest in dressage

172

training (especially in the type of work required for jumpers), and to gain an appreciation of the importance of this training in negotiating a course. The strong emphasis in this country on encouraging junior riders is giving a broader and broader base on which the team can rely for its future members. These classes for junior riders include flat work at all gaits as well as jumping over higher and more difficult fences and combinations with trickier turns than you will get on any other equitation course.

In this class the flat phase is run first. The flat phase is demanding. You are required to execute a sitting, ordinary, and extended trot, and an ordinary, strong, and counter canter. There is a work-off on the flat. The top ten to twelve riders are selected to ride a course.

You must be a junior member of the USET to compete in the class.

A winner of five of these classes receives a bronze medal; of ten classes, a silver medal; of twenty classes a gold medal. Gold medal winners are asked to come to Gladstone, New Jersey, to receive instruction.

PREPARING FOR EQUITATION CLASSES

Medal and Maclay riders prepare for an A show. Both horses pictured here are young and were purchased within the last two years. Their riders are members of the Ox Ridge Hunt Club, where they and their horses have been training. Philip Ake did a great deal of the preliminary training, but neither horse has passed out of the "green" stage. This makes them especially fit as examples in this chapter, because you will be able to see the methods still being used to train them. The photographs were taken during lessons with Vicki Ake prior to the Ox Ridge Horse Show. Both Philip and Vicki spent several hours choosing the photographs to illustrate helpful points and giving the information for the captions.

I asked Vicki what she particularly looked for in a Medal, Maclay, or USET rider. "The rider should have progressed to the stage where he no longer releases and no longer overjumps with his body," she said. "His horse should be obedient and supple so that he comes off his fences on whichever lead the rider asks or else changes leads within a stride or two after the fence. The greener a horse is, the more difficult it is to make a rider spend the needed time in preparing for the class. The performance itself, in the ring, should be unhurried and methodical. This not only means during the course, but right through to the exit out of the gate. The rider has to have a lot of self-discipline. And then there's the element of showmanship as opposed to horsemanship. You have to know how to cover up an error if one occurs. I have seen a rider with showmanship win over someone who had far better horsemanship, just because he knew how to mask a mistake." If you watch Vicki give a lesson, you see that she demands the self-discipline and the best both horse and rider can give.

Softening a Horse

Draw reins are used here on this roan mare to try to get more suppleness in her back and neck. (They should only be used by experienced riders.)

The mare is beginning to engage now as the rider goes into a posting trot.

She is starting to soften before her canter departure.

Then she breaks into a canter. (There is still slight resistence, however.) The softening process was helped by a lot of work making transitions from a trot to a canter and back to a sitting trot again. Interest was sustained by serpentines and figure eights at both a trot and a canter.

The extended trot increases the suppleness in a horse.

Here the horse is coming through on the left lead, changing to the right lead from the rear. The rider (who you can see is twisting a little in the saddle) is using her seat to influence the hindquarters.

In the air in a flying change. The horse is changing behind and is about to change in front, which is the correct way to execute the change of lead.

The final phase: the horse has almost completed the change to the left lead. He is coming up and carrying himself in the air for that stride. The rider is sitting in balance and straight.

A forward transition into a halt. The horse and rider are softening and doing the halt together. Her hands are good—soft, with the fingers open and relaxed. This is bringing the horse's head down, accepting the bit. Her knees are close to him, squeezing him forward to the halt. The horse's hind legs, still in motion, are coming under his body.

Normally, when a horse is circling to the right (clockwise) putting him on the "track to the right" with your right leg toward the center of the ring, you would take a right lead. If he takes a countercanter, he will take a left lead when he is on the right track. Here the leading left forefoot is hitting the earth for a countercanter.

The first fences were taken at a trot. Although the trot was a bit more extended than the rider wanted here, the motion and the jump were both good. Her horse did push from behind.

At the start of the lesson, four fences were taken on a single straight line. Gradually the number was increased until the horse was working through the course, which included a combination.

The horse here anticipated his fence, taking off a little too early. But the rider is right with him.

Immediately after the fence where he took off too early, the rider brought her horse to a halt. This was done both to discipline him and to check his rushing on other fences. It is a calming technique that works well with this horse.

When a horse takes over ahead of a fence, it is helpful to stop him *before* the obstacle. Here the rider has stopped in front of the fence and is just starting to walk on again. He is a strong horse, but the rider plays him to where she wants him. You need hands as good as hers to handle such a horse.

Now the horse is waiting for his fence. He and the rider have a fluid motion as they take it together. The rider's following hands rather than the looped rein of a beginning position are an indication of her experience.

This is an ugly looking fence with a regular brush in front of sheep hurtle wings. The horse had refused it twice before this picture was snapped. As you can see, the rider did not give him a chance to get out of it this time. The horse came into it looking, but the rider waited and waited, and when he finally took it, she stayed with him—very difficult under the circumstances. He made it, too. It is the waiting that is the hard part in approaching a new obstacle. It takes patience and finesse on the rider's part.

Here he takes the same fence with confidence in his ability to handle it. Again the rider is with him, balanced in the middle of her horse.

The rider is looking left toward her next fence. Her right leg is coming back. You can see an indication that the horse is beginning to come down on the left lead to complete the turn. Again, the rider's position is good.

12

Hunter Under Saddle, Working Hunter

The hunt conjures up a picture of well-dressed Englishmen in scarlet coats riding superbly schooled horses over the tailored English countryside. The horses are beautiful. They take fences gracefully and easily. They go on willingly, quietly, forever and ever, never missing a fence.

The great stone house of an Irish stud farm bordered a courtyard large enough for a Roman chariot race. Among the hundreds of stalls, one section had fine wood paneling, "loose" stalls the size of a normal bedroom for people, inhabited by fine-boned mares. The ears pricked on each sculptured head as I passed, the large eyes seemed to ask, "Have you come to take us on the hunt?" "We have seventeen horses we hunt two or three times a week during the season," the manager said. "There's no rougher country than you'll find here in Ireland. There's not an obstacle these horses won't take. Put them to a ten-foot wall, and they'd try to get over!" He made his point, but my mind conjured up what would happen to his horse on such a wall, and I didn't like the picture.

Yet this is the ideal type horse a judge looks for in the show ring—courage, quietness, steadiness, all this and much more. Your horse needs the stamina for a hunt in an Irish countryside. He needs beauty that speaks of conformation, from perfect legs to deep chest. In a hunter class, the way the horse moves, his long, swinging stride, has great importance. There are many kinds of hunter classes, but the hunter "type" is most likely to place high in every one. In actual practice, the horses found in the hunt field don't do well as a rule in the show ring and vice versa. The horse used for hunting is usually a more durable animal than the show-ring type.

TYPE OF HUNTER

Large horses tend to impress more than small ones, so that horses over sixteen hands tend to do better in under saddle classes than those less than that magic number. Finer-boned horses often do well in this type of class, but they still need the deep chest and strong hindquarters that speak of strength and endurance. Your hunter does not necessarily have to be a Thoroughbred. A properly built horse of other breeds can compete with success here. Quarter Horses are being bred more and more to the standard required. Many a Saddlebred, trained as a hunter, does well. Ponies, because they have short, choppy strides, are seldom entered in under-saddle classes. Your horse should be chestnut, black, brown, or gray. Grays have a slight edge, as a rule, because they stand out among other colors. The tendency to pin grays showed distinctly in one class in a recent National Horse Show at Madison Square Garden. The entire class, except one, were grays. The one chestnut took a ribbon.

TYPE OF CLASS

Hunter under saddle is on the flat—no jumps. A lot of hunting does not involve jumping. Some riders join the "gate brigade" and skip the fences. Under saddle and hack classes test horses for this type of riding.

HOW SHOULD YOU RIDE?

Ride with light contact. This means you feel the bit, but the reins shouldn't be tight. You can see for yourself by watching a class who has the right hands for contact. When a rider sets his hands on the withers and never moves them, he cannot be feeling the movement of the bit, even though he might have light hands. If you see the reins go slack and tight beside the neck, the rider does not have contact. A horse who shoots his nose in the air or tucks his chin to his chest is resisting in his way a rider's hard hands. As your horse's head moves forward, your hands shift forward with it; but if your hands are resilient, they also feel the release of tension as his head moves back and they shift backward to maintain a feel of the bit. Since the horse is being judged, not you, you must do everything you can to show him off at his finest. The better your balance as a rider, the easier it is for him to look balanced. The better your aids, the more quickly

He is a big-boned 16.2 hands, but when she rode him in a hunter under saddle class on Cape Cod, she felt as if she were on a pony. All the rest of the horses were 17 hands!

he responds to commands from the judge, and the more willing he appears as a hunter.

WHAT ARE YOU ASKED TO DO?

The walk, trot, and canter both directions are required. Only one speed of the trot is expected. You can be asked to take a canter from both a trot and a walk. The hand gallop is usually asked for at the end of a class when the judge is close to picking his winners. You can have eight horses galloping at the same time, and you know how this inspires a horse to move on. So be sure yours is well "in hand." A soft, pleasing halt and slowing down the same way indicate good manners. Of course, he should back straight, willingly, and with the right amount of flexion.

IS THE CLASS DIFFICULT?

It is more difficult than pleasure horse or road hack. This one counts toward championship points and those do not. More is expected of your horse. A horse must be sound for any pleasure horse, hack, or under saddle

The quiet, well-mannered hunter is the one who wins. You should have the same relaxed attitude that you see here in both horse and rider before the class.

class. A judge considers type and movement whether it is a conformation class or not. Here the angle of your horse's head and neck is important. They should be extended rather than arched or tucked. A horse who carries his head in a proper set position looks nice. If you expect a ribbon won in this class to count toward championship points, you have to ride over fences in the same show.

Working Hunter

Working hunter includes all the categories, from under saddle to jumping. However, a class that simply says in your catalogue, "Working Hunter," is going to be over fences. The majority of hunter classes will be jumping classes. Hunter classes in a ring differ greatly from a hunt. In fact, many show horses never go on a hunt in their lives. A ring will give you better turf than the countryside, but in most respects it is more difficult to ride in a ring than cross-country. Your ring course will have sharper turns. You will be expected to put in a nearly perfect performance in a very few minutes. One A show for a junior division had a course that took one minute and forty-five seconds. That's not long. Every second in the ring counts. A horse may not have to be quite as quiet in a ring as in the countryside, because he will be easier to control with the sight of those barriers all around him. Some shows, however, have excellent facilities that include a stretch

At some shows the hunt course is in a field. The eight fences will have variety, but all could be found in the hunt field. All will have wings.

of field or woods that is easily viewed by the judge. This has the advantage of giving your horse a long hunt course.

WHAT THE JUDGE LOOKS FOR

First he looks for the special horse that has brilliance, or quality, style, a way of carrying himself. You can be sure this includes manners. A horse who takes the bit, rushes his fences, lays back his ears, or has to pull himself together after he lands does not have the smooth, unmarred round.

Then there's pace. This means evenness, smoothness, and unchanged tempo all the way around. Horses tend to speed up toward the end of a course. Try to pick up the pace you want at the start and maintain just that speed the whole way. You can take quite a fast round, even in a junior division, as long as your horse is under control. Consistency is important. Even a slow, measured pace, if your horse jumps well that way, is acceptable. But most judges prefer a faster, energetic pace. A judge may rate pace separately with a number on his card and use this number to break ties. Other judges, though they notice pace, do not rate it as highly.

A horse who is easy to manage has an advantage. This is one reason why you see so many snaffle bits in hunter classes. This type bit seems to say, "I'm easy to handle." But if you need more leverage for control, move on to a pelham or double bridle, or, if you still want a single rein, to a Kimberwicke.

Movement is important. A horse should seem to flow over the ground. The low, swinging gait that wastes little energy is the ideal.

The arc over each fence is marked by the judge. The horse who takes off the same distance ahead of a fence as he lands afterward, who has a smooth clean arc through the air, is a beautiful sight. The top of his arc will be right over the center of the fence. Touches and knockdowns are inefficiencies, but many judges don't even count rubs if the arc is good and the fence isn't dangerous. The fence should be jumped in the middle. The way a horse arches his neck and back are part of the overall picture of his jump. His head and neck should extend for balance. A judge notes if he tucks his legs nicely. He shouldn't drop a leg because this hints at a bad fall if he tangles with a fence.

His conformation will count. If he is put together properly he is more likely to have stamina and give you a comfortable ride. Normally Thoroughbreds win. Years of racing have built stamina into the breed, which give strength and endurance in the hunt field. Racing records on Thoroughbreds show a direct relationship between conformation and a horse's ability to go distance. Your horse must be supple, strong, and in excellent condition with solid weight on him.

The horse (not the rider) is judged in hunter classes. He should make the same perfect arc over every fence.

He must take the fence in the middle. The fence will be under the center of his arc. The judge watches how he uses himself: his legs tuck under him; they are even; he has a nice arch to his back and neck; he uses his neck and head well for balance. This is the start of a fine jump.

You can be called back to jog for soundness as in this class at Madison Square Garden.

KINDS OF CLASSES

You will find names such as Working Hunter Over Fences, Green Working Hunter, Pony Working Hunter, Novice Hunter. All are over fences. You will also find some with the word *conformation* in the title, such as Green Conformation Hunter. Part of the points in these classes are based on conformation (usually forty percent, but it might be only twenty-five percent, and can go higher). In conformation classes, the judge calls back the ones he has chosen, lines them up on the basis of performance, then changes the order on the basis of conformation.

Class specifications tell you the height of the fences. They will be lower in pony, green, maiden, and novice hunter classes than in the others. You can use prize money for a key; the higher the prizes, the tougher the competition, and usually it means the higher the fences, too.

TYPES OF FENCES

They will represent fences you might find in a hunt field. Rails will be natural wood, though you can get stripes on one for a railroad crossing. Brush and walls, gates and chicken coops are common. You may get aikens, banks, ditches, and water. The types of jumps vary in different parts of the country. There is always an in and out, and often two of them, one with a single stride, the next fence two strides away. Rarely are the fences over four and a half feet, and usually they are between three and four feet. There's not much difference between fences in small unrecognized shows and large, recognized ones, except in height. (Usually they run three feet six inches in unrecognized shows rather than four feet.) All the fences will have wings.

HOW TO MAKE A HUNTER ROUND

Memorize the course. Know the turns, the order, the look of it. Excitement is a memory-mixer, and you don't want to forget. Don't stand waiting at the in gate building up tension for the last five minutes before your round. Warm up your horse. At least keep moving around to keep your mind—and your horse's—off what lies ahead.

Enter the ring smartly, looking straight ahead. Put on your business-like attitude. A judge can tell a lot about your horse with his first look. Make a large entrance circle, coming out of it at a canter on the lead you want for the start of the course. A mother who had become a professional show-watcher in the three years her daughter had been riding in rated

Usually there is a stone wall.

There will be an in and out.

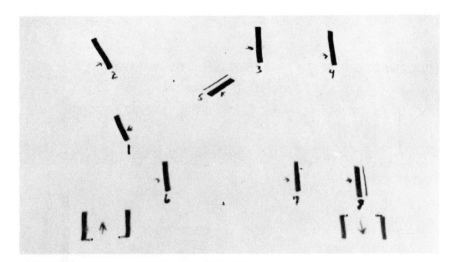

The diagram of the course may not be fancy, but it shows the order of the fences and the direction they are to be taken. This is the diagram of a hunter course at an A show. You can see the arrows on the in and out gates, as well as the eight fences.

A hunt course set up and waiting for you, the audience eager and watching. Just to look at the ring gives you the feeling of what it is like at a big show.

Make a large entrance circle before you start the course.

shows, watched one young girl make her entrance circle. "Just look at that," she said in disgust. "She's making a tiny circle. Why didn't she take this chance to show off her horse to the judge by making a nice big one?"

Now come straight into the middle of your first fence. You want that nice line that lets your horse take off easily for every fence. If you have a change of direction, you will make a flying change of leads so that you maintain the smooth look to your round. In maiden, novice, and junior classes, you may stay at a counter canter or even cross canter without penalty, but you must not break into a trot. A judge likes to see a change of lead. Usually a cross canter or counter canter counts off only at top shows, or if the fence following is poor as a result. The correct lead (or a counter canter) does look better, however, and usually guarantees a better fence. It is better to do

Maintain the same "hunter" pace throughout the course. Don't be afraid to make wide curves. Here the horse is moving freely, without racing, in a good hunter approach. He is alert as the rider holds him on light contact.

that than to attempt a flying change, miss it, and mess up your whole round. Since Decision won't make flying changes without cross-cantering, my daughter doesn't change leads with him even in regular hunter classes. She figures it won't count off much for being on the wrong lead. It doesn't; he still wins ribbons. So decide the way your horse will have the smoothest round. Make everything as easy for him as you can. Don't rush your round. Go deep into your corners and make wide turns where there is space for them.

If you are inexperienced, let your horse take the course for himself. When you have show know-how, watch everyone else with care. See how the good riders cut down the number of strides in a combination to get the smooth look. Watch where they place their entrance circles, how they approach fences. Decide whether your horse can take the same number of strides between fences as theirs do. More and more you will enjoy the challenge of figuring out how to take the course. It can be more absorbing than winning.

Junior classes will give you stiff competition. You will find many riders such as this with the ability as well as the horse that can win.

A Judge's Card from an Open Working Hunter Class. Each judge develops his own system for marking hunter rounds. Here is the code this judge used: On each of the nine fences

G   good overall fence
cc/   cross canter
SBD   slight drawback at fence
AG   average to good fence
sc   slightly close to fence in takeoff
.   rubbed fence
Fo   loose fold over fence
C   close to fence in takeoff
U   jumped at base of fence (under fence)
Hd   head (tosses head, carries it at angle, etc.)
H   hit deep into fence
SH   shoot at fence (big move)
Ä   rubbed fence back/front
R   rail down
S   refusal
FL   flat over fence
SR   slight reach over fence
TW   twist
DB   horse draws back before fence
Conformation indicates what kind of mover:
A—excellent
B—good
C—average
Manners and way of going: numerical score 0–100 based on performance. Total includes all of these in the order judge sees it.

HUNTERS AND JUMPERS

CONDITIONS

CLASS

CLASS 202—Open Working Hunters   Entry Fee $5.00
Open to all. The Judges are to pick the horses, apparently the
most agreeable mounts to hounds, the main consideration being
manners, even hunting pace, way of going, style of jumping and
hunting soundness. Ticks will not be scored unless the faults of
bad jumping. Conformation will not be considered. Full Championship Points. Fences 4'.
: 6 Ribbons—$30, $20, $15, $10, $5, $5

First 489 Second 759 Third 1019 Fourth 756 Fifth 748

Sixth 491 Reserve 761

*Judges will select and mark "RESERVE" one more
horse than the number of awards in any class to
provide for the contingency of a disqualification.*

No.	1	2	3	4	5	6	7	8	9	10	Conformation	Manners and Way of Going	Performance	Total
1019	G	G	AG	G	G	G	AG	AG	G		B	(70)		
792	AG	FG	SG	G	G	AG	C	AG	G		B	20		489
756	G	AG	AG	G	G	G	AC	G	AG		B	(60)		
780	G	4	S	3	SC	G	G	G	G		Bc	SG		759
491	AG	4	AG	G	AG	G	AG	AG	G		B	(40)		1019
819	A	B	C	AG	G	AG	AG	G	G		B	R		
792	AG	4	G	AP	G	G	AG	G	G		Bc	30		
779	AG	A	SG	AG	AG	G	G	R	G		Bc	R		
761	G	W	H	G	G	G	AG	AG	G		Bc	35		756
681	G	SR	G	G	G	G	G	G	G		Bc	25		
489	G	G	G	G	G	G	G	G	G		B	(90)		748
748	G	AG	AG	G	G	AG	AG	G	AG		B	(used)		
793	G	AG	AG	G	G	DB	SD	AG			B	31		491
759	G	G	G	AG	AG	G	G	G	AG		B	(used)		
														761

HODGES BADGE COMPANY   53 Smith Place, Cambridge, Mass. 02138

205

13

The Jumper Division

WHAT KIND OF HORSE?

A horse who thrills to jumping, who hates to touch his fences, who is responsive and willing, makes the finest jumper. His handiness, the ease with which he maneuvers tight corners and changes pace, add to his value. More jumpers are Thoroughbreds than any other breed, but some famous jumpers have been ponies, standing less than 14.2 hands, so don't rule out your horse as a potential jumper either because of his size or his breed. Jumper classes depend on two things: your horse's ability to clear his fences and his skill at speed on a tight course. The look of him matters not at all. Pinto or pony, cold-blooded or "hot," no one cares—if he can jump.

Yorke Spring is a jumper, a rather strange one at that. Beauty is hardly his emblem, even when groomed to a shine and with his mane pulled. With some horses there's just not much you can do to cover up what they really are. But he is an audience-pleaser just the same, not because of his big feet, but because of his jumping style. Few are the horses who come into a fence *his* way. Just as he arrives, he stalls, then gathers himself and bounds over. The audience gasps. Everyone loves the underdog and he sure looks like a loser; so when he makes it, cheers follow his course. Oddly enough, he is a steady jumper even if he doesn't look like one. And he wins, too.

Custom even eases up on the looks of tack and rider. They don't count toward points. One young rider I know always wears a turtleneck sweater with his breeches and boots, which is hardly conventional, but he feels at ease that way. You'll probably feel better in riding clothes, though, rather than flouting custom and standing out as the odd one among other riders. Also, riding clothes have been designed to make riding comfortable. Your pride in your horse will show in his tack and grooming.

206

A competent horse and junior rider making a good jump.

WHAT MAKES A JUMPER CLASS?

A jumper is penalized for hitting his fences and not for the kind of horse he is. Your hunter must have style and a pleasant way of going, a smooth pace and nice manners. *He* is being judged. A jumper is judged by *performance* over fences, on how good he is, not on how he does it. A horse *can* be both a hunter and a jumper, though the styles for each division are quite different. There are few horses, however, who have the temperament to change from one division to the other.

HOW MANY CLASSES DO YOU ENTER?

You wouldn't enter a horse in both hunter and jumper classes in the same show, however, because it would be too hard on him to jump that much, even if he did have the temperament for it. You could be called back for the jumpoffs in a jumper class. Each jumpoff is like an extra class. You want to have a chance at the stake classes and in the championship class at the end of the show, and a tired horse doesn't have a chance. With junior riders, you could enter equitation classes as well as hunter *or* jumper classes.

WHAT KIND OF COURSE?

The fences are created out of someone's imagination, and at times you would think they came from science fiction. They are supposed to shock, surprise, and challenge a horse—and they do just that. The optical illusion on a panel or with stripes on the post and rails is a glaring eyecatcher at shows. Modern designs rear up from walls. Nor do course designers depend only on the eye for confusion. Distance is the real challenge. The varying strides between the in and out and among combinations take skill to maneuver. The long approach on a straightaway before a single fence demands calm minds in both horse and rider. Odd fences are legal, even anxiously sought by course planners. A single combination might have post and rails, an oxer that goes higher with each rail of a spread, and one that drops with the third rail. Or a high paneled coop might be substituted for an oxer. Square oxers, one of the most difficult of fences, come in various forms. As if all this weren't enough, difficult turns and changes of direction add to the trickiness of jumper division courses. Throw on top of this that most classes add the element of time, so that speed becomes a factor. Small wonder the crowds come to see jumpers; small wonder the horses in this division are some of the strongest, most courageous, and best bred in the horse world.

HOW HIGH ARE THE FENCES?

Five feet is not unusual, even at small shows. The fences will begin around four feet, but when the jumpoff is finished, they are higher and broader. At the "big" shows in places such as Madison Square Garden, or the Devon Show where you have international competitions, fences hit and even pass the six-foot mark.

The height and spread of fences has about reached the capacity of the horse. New challenges lie in the difficult course, the one designed for the

A plank fence that creates an optical illusion.

A long run to the next fence—difficult to hold down his anticipation.

Combinations vary in difficulty. They can have odd spacing between the fences . . .

Or tough turns as in this course at Madison Square Garden.

handy horse who can adjust his stride and maneuver quickly. More riders are reaching for the Grand Prix. The challenge of jumping a course with difficult distances between the fences, a course that demands intelligence, skill, and quick thinking, is becoming the goal of designers.

"People should realize the level of the Grand Prix and reach for it," Tibby Hunt says. "A 'hot' horse just isn't it anymore. A well mannered, quiet, workable temperament is what wins today." Now that the fences can hardly get wider or broader, "the ribbons are going to have to go to the riders who don't make mistakes." This is the coming challenge in showing.

This puts less emphasis on the large horse. In fact, "A horse around 16.2 hands is proving the best size for all-round jumping," Ray Moloney, instructor at Round Hill Stables in Greenwich, Connecticut, says. "He can get out of a tight in and out. Yet he can stretch for the long stride, too. Now tell me, if you ask a horse who is seventeen hands to take a four-foot vertical fence at the start of a one stride in and out, where will he land?" Ray asks. "That's making the smaller, sixteen-hand horse come into his own."

Spreads range from a few feet to eight feet. You get different types of square oxers. A nice line to the bit indicates good hands.

A high wall seems to be part of every course. Here it is equivalent to the bank jump.

Tight turns and galloping are a big part of jumper classes.

TABLES I AND II

"Tables" for jumping are listed in the AHSA rule book. The ones you need to know are I and II, although there are others. Table I has penalties for touches as well as knock-downs, but does not use time for judging winners. (These are often called the "touch" classes.) Mistakes, known as faults, are valued by points. The worse the fault, the higher the points. So the winner is the one with the *lowest* points or faults. It is worse to hit the fence with the forelegs than the hind legs, so a tick or rub, or touch (all terms are used) counts one fault with the forelegs, but only one-half a fault with the hind legs. "What if your horse hits with both front and back," a child about to enter a class asked. Her instructor said quickly, "Only the bigger fault counts. It would be only one fault." A horse who knocks down a jump gets four faults. The term *disobedience* is used, too. It means a refusal or stopping (called loss of forward motion). Running out on (evading) a jump counts as much as a disobedience. Faults add up quickly for a disobedience or evasion. The first time counts three faults, the second time six faults, and the third time you are eliminated. There are three ways to be eliminated: one, by a disobedience or evasion; two, by not crossing the starting line within one minute after entering the ring; three, by you or your horse falling. Ties are broken by jumpoffs in which the fences are made higher and broader. If you learn Table I by heart, you'll have less trouble remembering that everything else comes under Table II.

Under Table II only knock-downs count. Time becomes a factor in most of the sections. (It doesn't count in section 5 [Knock Down and Out] or section 6 [The Puissance].) Scoring is the same as in Table I. It is easier to remember at what phase time becomes a factor in breaking ties if you subtract one number from the section number of sections 1, 2, and 3. In section 3, ties are broken in the second jumpoff by time; in section 2, ties are broken in the first jumpoff by time; in section 1, ties are broken by time while riding the first round. Remember, however, the rules are constantly updated, so that you need a rule book to keep up with current points.

A shorthand reference for Tables I and II follows.

AHSA Table I
Touches and knockdowns count
Touches: ½ fault—hind legs
              1 fault—forelegs
Knockdown: 4 faults
Disobedience: refusing to jump or loss of forward motion
Disobedience or Evasion: 1st time: 3 faults
                            2nd time: 6 faults
                            3rd time: elimination
Elimination: 3rd disobedience or evasion
                failure to cross starting line within one minute of entering ring
                fall of horse or rider
Ties: successive jumpoffs over fences higher and broader
Time is not a factor

AHSA Table II   Touches are not penalized   Time Counts
                 Scoring same as in Table I

Section 1: Time taken to complete the course is used to break ties

Section 2: Jumping faults and penalties (seconds you exceed Time Allowed for finishing the course) are added together
            Ties: time decides in 1st jumpoff

Section 3: Add together jumping faults and penalties (for exceeding Time Allowed) to get winners in both 1st round and 1st jumpoff

Ties: time decides in 2nd jumpoff between horses with clean rounds or equal faults

AHSA Table II
Section 4: Fault and Out
Your Round ends with the first fault you get
Points awarded (instead of faults)

    1 point for knocked down obstacle

    2 points when clear obstacle

Signal sounds when you knock it down, or when you get to the Time Allowed. You still take the next fence and your total time is counted unil your horse's forefeet touch the ground. But this last obstacle doesn't give you any points.

Object: to jump as many fences as possible in Time Allowed.

If you finish the course and the signal hasn't been given, start again.

AHSA Table II
Section 5: Knock Down and Out
Winner is one who clears the most fences without a fault.
No time.

AHSA Table II
Section 6: The Puissance
Strength competition
Begins with 6 fences
For each jumpoff: 2 fences are removed until only 2 are left

    one is a spread

    one is a vertical wall

Increase height and spread until get winner
No time.

Table II has many sections. Other popular ones are Gambler's Choice and Take Your Own Line. For Gambler's Choice, ten fences of varying difficulty are set up in the ring. Their value ranges from ten to one hundred points. The rider is supposed to earn as many points as he can by jumping the fences of his choice within the time limit (which is around a minute). He can go in any order, in either direction, but cannot take a fence more than twice. If he knocks one down, it doesn't count.

Take Your Own Line is similar. There are ten fences, each to be taken once. The rider may go in any order, but the one who gets over them fastest with the fewest faults wins.

KNOW THE COURSE

Always know your course before you start. Learn it, and then walk it,

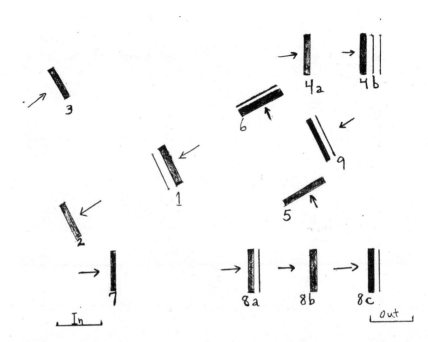

The diagram of a jumper course at an A show. The same diagram was used for three classes: class 64, Preliminary Jumpers; class 68, Amateur Owner Jumpers; class 56, Junior Jumpers. Table II, section 2 rules applied to classes 64 and 68; Table I rules to class 56. When time was a factor, the course was to be completed within seventy seconds. In the jumpoff, fences numbered 1, 4a and b, 6, 8a, b, and c, and 9 would be used.

and then think about it. No matter how well a horse jumps, *he* can't follow the course. Debby found it out the hard way. This was her first show. She had developed skill as a rider even if she was only ten years old, but the last thing she expected was to ride in a show, because her parents couldn't afford the entry fees or proper riding clothes. Someone else gave Debby her chance, someone who liked children and had the right horse for her. Debby rode in borrowed clothes. Her new friend paid the entrance fees. Never in her life had Debby been so excited. Since her horse had been in scores of shows, all she had to do was sit quietly so that she didn't interfere with him. He did it almost perfectly, with only one small rub, which should have given him second place. Only Debby's excitement muddled her thinking. She went off course. In spite of her mistake, she came in sixth. How did Debby feel? Well, it *was* her first show, and she came out of that class the happiest girl around.

LEADS

"You take the course into consideration when you take your first lead,"

A rider must know several strides before a fence whether to steady his horse or move him on to get him to the takeoff spot exactly right. The high fences of a jumper course demand greater precision in hitting the correct takeoff point. Poor timing runs the risk of refusal.

Tibby Hunt said one day at a show. "Leads are important from the point of view of balance," she continued. "Say you are going over that fence in the middle there." She pointed to a single fence before a change of direction in the course in the show ring in front of us. "You would know you wanted to be on your left lead when you landed. Your horse might land on the left lead a lot better if he is on the left hand when he takes off. His balance might be better that way. With other horses, it might not make a big difference. You might make a flying change after the fence. You expect a good jumper to make them easily. It is important to know your horse so you can make the most of his ability."

RIDING THE COURSE

Begin with training your horse to maneuver easily. Practice with tight courses at home. Before you enter the ring plan how you will ride the course. In a hunter class you have more time between obstacles to figure out what to do. In a jumper class, you may need to hold your horse back for one stride and then give him impulse for the next stride.

Suppose you have a square oxer where you know your horse cannot see the second bar until he is in the air—you can help him by bringing him in close to the fence for his takeoff. This way his natural arc will reach beyond the middle of the first rail, so that he won't need to stretch so far for the second one after he is airborne.

Tom Kranz, Director of Longacres Riding Camp, said about his favorite jumper, China Heart, "He will try anything. I remember the first fence at the New York State Fair in Syracuse. It was a square oxer, the first section solid plywood, so you couldn't see the second section five feet away until you rose in the air. When China Heart got up and over the first part, he saw the single bar way out there in front of him. Sometimes I think a horse has something extra within himself to get a stronger effort when he is already in the air. It's something people just don't have. You can't get more spring after your feet leave the ground. This time, when China Heart saw what was needed, he actually grunted deep inside. I could see him stretch himself, feel him reaching for all he was worth. And he got over that second bar."

The better your eye for distance, the better your sense of timing for fences will be. The more you can make yourself think intelligently while on the course, the better your chances are to win. You must be flexible, too. You need to be quick to deal with the unforeseen circumstance, the bad jump, your horse's temperament.

Sue, who had just turned thirteen, was going to ride China Heart in a junior jumper class. China Heart is a most unpredictable, erratic horse. This particular day he came into the ring and started off like a cyclone. He took his first fence at an all-out gallop. What should Sue have done? She did her best; she rode it out. But if she had a few more years of showing behind her, been a little more flexible in her plans, she would have thought, "He'll never make the fences at this pace. I'm out of it unless I get control. What'll I do? Stop! That's three faults. He'll knock down half the fences at this pace and that's a lot more faults." But how many people would think after the first fence that the smart thing to do with a rushing horse was to stop? Sue took her chances. China Heart knocked down four fences. On another day, Sue rode China Heart to a championship.

When you are riding for time, you have to figure out how short a turn your own horse can make, and still gather himself for the next fence. You

A high vertical fence will have a sharper arc than a spread. The horse takes off closer than he would on a low jump (under four feet). He must bend well.

have to judge your competition, too. "I noticed in a jumpoff that you might be able to cut inside one of the eliminated fences and so save time," a show rider said to me after he won a class. "No one else thought it was possible, so I won."

"Yorke Spring likes to look things over," Tom Kranz says. "When you are riding for time with him you have to decide: 'I know Yorke can turn fast and take one stride on that corner, but if he does, he will come right up on the fence. He can make it, but he won't be able to think about it and then I risk a refusal.' If it were China Heart I was riding, I would know I needed more space. I'd have to figure whether he could make the corner at

An oxer with a wide spread demands a different jumping style. The arc will be flatter. The horse here makes this one look easy.

that angle, not whether he could make the fence. I have to think ahead and plan for China Heart. Yorke is steadier; you don't have to be as good a rider to win with him." This is knowing your horses, their temperament, their ability, their agility.

STRIDES AND FENCES

You need to memorize the number of strides between an in and out and in combinations. A single stride in and out is twenty-four feet apart.

A two stride in and out is thirty-six feet apart. With a four-foot vertical fence, it is thirty-three feet. Three strides between a combination is forty-eight feet. You can take two feet more or less on either side of these distances by shortening or lengthening your horse's stride. If it varies more than that, you are in for a tough time. "I drill my riders when they are walking around relaxing their horses," Tom Kranz says. "I throw numbers at them and they have to come back quick with how many strides, or how they would alter their horses' strides to make an in and out. It's something you just have to know if you are going to jump courses."

You have to pace your course. A combination may give you two strides between the first two fences and one stride between the second and third. You discover this when you pace it, and then figure out how you'll ride it beforehand. A long spread will take you further into the in and out, and you will be moving more quickly from it than a vertical. If there are two normal strides after a spread, you will decide when you walk the course how you will take the combination. If the two strides are thirty-six feet, you'd decide to take it in two strides. If you had to make an adjustment

A combination can be a double or a treble.

Triple bars can be more difficult than they look. *Photo by Tarrance.*

because of your horse's ability, you would make it at the first obstacle. For example, if your horse had an unusually long stride, you would meet the first obstacle at the base to shorten the distance he would cover in the air, and then you still might have to steady him or take back in the middle of the combination. Only if there was no other alternative would you try to take the thirty-six-feet in one stride. Not only could that mean a knockdown, it could be dangerous as well.

Unusual obstacles, such as banks, ditches and water, must be taken at most big shows. Here is an excellent jump over water.

Ox Ridge Hunt Club has a jump that challenges horses to the utmost: this bank. In the series here the top photo shows a horse on the bank jump at almost the same instant as a different horse—close up—takes it.

FENCES AT ANGLES

In time classes, you know you will jump fences at an angle because it is one of the easier ways to cut the number of strides between a couple of obstacles. Sometimes, however, you have to make a decision about whether to jump at an angle or not. Tibby Hunt discussed this problem with me. "You may have to turn after a fence. Your horse may jump the fence neater on a straight line than at an angle. So you go over it straight and turn afterwards. But if you know your horse, know he can take a fence easily at an angle, you'd do that instead and save the time."

POSITION AS AN AID

"One of the most difficult fences is a square oxer after a long run," Tibby went on. "Sometimes you put your horse in your hand by using your leg. This way you can check his stride to slow him and to put him on his hindquarters. Then he jumps round, through his back, enabling him to clear the fence well with both his front and hind feet. If he gets going too fast he may take it flat and cause a knockdown.

"You get back in the saddle to set him up for a vertical fence. With a quick turn and a vertical, I get back and upright, and, at the last minute, forward very fast for the fence. For a spread or a long fence, I will be forward coming into it and be there already when he is starting over it. Of course, I am being general. Many decisions of how to ride a specific fence depend on the rest of the course. Actually, you tend to ride forward more on a hunter than on a jumper." She added soberly. "This is all difficult, and technical. It takes practice and experience to do it right."

TIME VS. FAULTS

At one of the top shows, in the final ride-off in which time decided in the case of equal faults, a young man completed the course in several seconds less than any previous competitor. He had only ½ a fault, the fewest yet. The last rider had three fences to go when a loud voice pierced the hush of the crowd. "Don't ride for time, Jan. I was wrong. Ride for no faults." Jan slowed slightly for the tricky fence just ahead. She made it without a fault. The next fence, too, passed clear beneath her horse's hoofs. The last fence now! It was a huge plank obstacle. She made it without a fault. Her time came in a fraction over that of the young man. She had gambled on perfection and won. This type of decision must be made again and again in top competition. That's why you have to know your horse and his ability.

A good position so often results in a good jump.

A rider's form can affect a horse's balance. Even in a jumper class you see excellent examples of good form.

A good rider can use her position, her hands, and her experience to help her horse win the blue. She did!

Nearly perfect form—and look at the eagerness of her horse! *Photo by Wilkinson*.

14

Some of the Finer Moments of Showing

A young man entered his first open jumper class in an A show. The tension he felt showed in his bright eyes, controlled voice, and the fact that he left his friends earlier than usual before the class. Some of his tension communicated itself to his horse. There was one refusal, followed by a perfect jump. Two fences later, a second refusal. And finally, on an easy fence, a third refusal. After he had gone over it, taking it as a schooling fence, he turned around, faced the judge, and tipped his hat. He was the first one in the show to make the gesture, and he did it with real respect. The sportsmanship of the horse show world reveals itself in small gestures and large unselfishness that set it apart.

This same young man, waiting with anticipation for the stake class, now that he had faced the big fences once, took his horse out for a little exercise the following afternoon. To his dismay, his horse favored one leg. It was only a stone in his shoe, but even when the stone came out, a little of the hurt remained. They would not enter the stake class that night. Did he curse his luck? Not at all. He gave thanks for discovering the trouble and knowing his horse would be all right. A bond had grown up between him and his horse, so that love weighed mightier than a class or a ribbon or anything a show might offer. Yet it was showing that had created the bond.

The horse-show world has an international language. Not once, but over and over throughout the show season, you compete with riders from other nations. When you consider the expense of coming to a show, not just transportation and hotels for yourself, but the far higher cost of transportation and stables and grooms for your horses, you could expect the people who showed to be a bit high hat. I asked a rider from Ontario,

It takes courage to enter the open jumper class at an A show and compete with riders and horses as skilled as this.

Canada, if I might use his picture in a book. My timing was terrible. He had just come out of the ring and a groom had taken his horse. I thought it a good moment. What I didn't realize was that he was going to ride four other horses in the same class. Did he give me the impatient answer I deserved? Not at all. As he swung onto his next horse with only minutes to spare before his next round, he gave me a broad smile and a willing response. Here was a man absorbed in his job, pressed by time, trying to

Of course, winning is always a wonderful thing.

handle several green horses at once, and he could take time to be pleasant to a perfect stranger. The amazing thing about it is that everyone at the show responded in the same way.

When I asked Tibby Hunt, who had been in a lot more shows than I had even seen, who had just returned from the Florida circuit, what were some of the unusual benefits she found in showing, she, too, spoke about people. You get an insight into people from all over the world when you work side by side in the show field. "I know riders from Canada and England and even New Zealand," Tibby said. "I also have a friend from South Africa who is now training and showing in this country."

Perhaps Tom Kranz's showing career is not so unusual as it seems to me. There must be other riders who share his rise to the top, but I know of none who compressed it into such a few months of their lives. There's something of story book quality to the way it happened. At the core of the story is China Heart.

Tom had heard about China Heart. The gelding had jumped well at local shows. But who could have counted on terrible weather the day China Heart went up for sale at a bankruptcy auction? Only one other stable knew the horse's quality and it was in Rochester. The weather kept them home. This left Tom as the only buyer with enough money in his pocket and the knowledge in his heart of what the horse could do. So he came home with the horse that was to change his life.

"It seemed a shame to own a horse like China and never ride him yourself," Tom said. At that time Tom had already been Director of Longacres Riding Camp for several years. He hadn't been on a horse since he was sixteen, and even as a boy he had just hopped on and off horses for the fun of it. Not once had he had a lesson. A nearby instructor gave him four lessons. "I wanted to learn the basic position and how to post." Tom had never learned that. "My big advantage," he said, "was my willingness to ask questions so that I could find out the reasons why you did everything the instructor told you. Most of the campers seem afraid to ask and it hinders their progress."

Tom had another advantage, as I view it—he had "guts." He wasn't afraid to try, or make mistakes, or even to start his riding career on as difficult a horse as China Heart turned out to be. He had only been riding a few weeks when he entered his first show, a local one, in the open jumper class. That takes something special in a rider. You can raise your eyebrows if you want, but he won two firsts and third in that show! That was in November. During the winter he entered local shows, and China Heart was undefeated right through February. Once he beat a horse who had been on the Canadian Equestrian Team.

By March he dared a big show at the Saddle and Bridle Club in Buffalo, New York. "The salient feature of that show," he said, "was that

I didn't fall off." I always like Tom's modesty when he talks about showing. He won a third place in that show against the horses of quality he had feared as competitors.

At a show two weeks later he did fall off. "That's when I decided I needed lessons," he said. "I looked around at who was winning that day, and picked the woman who rode off with the most ribbons—that was Tibby Hunt." He had three lessons with her at that time.

Tom began riding a second horse he had bought, Yorke Spring. In the shows he rode both horses, taking ribbons and even championships. In September, when he hadn't been showing a year, he entered the New York State Fair at Syracuse, where he took two ribbons in preliminary jumpers. "That was the toughest show I had been in," Tom admitted. After that he went on to other shows, had more lessons, and became an old hand at showing.

Now you'd think that the reward was there, in winning so many ribbons his first year as a rider. But showing meant much more than that to Tom. You must remember he is a camp director, and that means involvement with youth. Right along with his own showing, he gave children a chance. In some shows he took a back seat and let young girls ride his prize horses in junior divisions. At first Longacres had a couple of stalls at local shows. Within the first year that number jumped to eight, and it is still rising. Inevitably Tom found himself schooling the girls who rode China Heart. "I enjoy teaching now even more than riding," Tom says. I looked at Sue Bell's eyes during an A show just before she entered a jumper class. She is one of Tom's most apt students. Anyone who likes children would have thrilled to the glow in her eyes, and it was Tom and China Heart who put it there.

One of the most pleasant things horses can do is bring a close relationship between parent and child. I met a young mother when her daughter was only a couple of years old. At that time the mother was the only person who could ride my Thoroughbred Mischief without having him run away with her. In the end she bought the horse and trained him so well to forget his racetrack background that even her daughter could ride him. "My daughter was fortunate," her mother admits, "because she had that natural talent that made her good right from the start. I think a child has to have it when she must compete with an adult rider, or she loses interest in horses." I'm not sure whether the young girl is so good because her mother knows so much or whether it is inherent in her. I've only seen her ride once, and she is good. She has her own Thoroughbred now and at twelve is earning his keep by teaching friends to ride. With this background, and a horse who could win, you'd expect to find her at the top shows in the East where she lives. But she likes Pony Club. And she likes eventing, which she does with her mother. Once in a while they enter local shows. At one of them a class

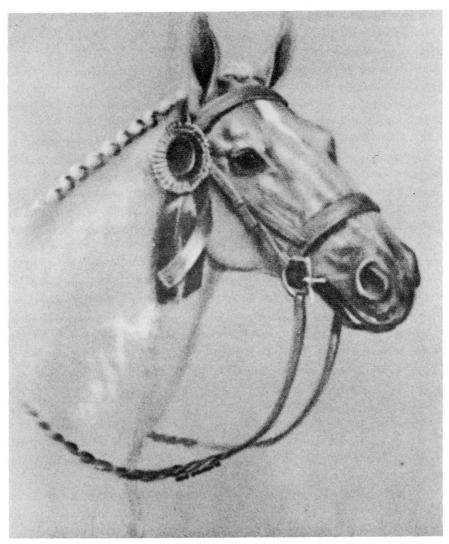

A horse she'll remember.

was offered in which one member of the family rode the outside hunt course and another member did the hacking in the ring. The mother's horse is big for a small twelve year old (it is sixteen hands), but her daughter had taken one ribbon with him in the show, so her mother let her ride him on the outside course. Her mother did the hacking part. They won the trophy. But the fun part was doing it together.

Not every story has a happy ending. Perhaps this is why showing molds riders to take the bitter with the sweet and smile when they take it. Debby

Totton was given a filly for Christmas. She was a double registered palomino Quarter Horse. The filly had lost its dam and Debby fed it with a bottle until it learned to drink from a bowl. All her life that mare loved to drink milk from a bowl. Because she was an orphan, the filly became "Debby's Orphy." As a yearling she won the 4-H Club show in Illinois. At two she won the State Championship for English Showmanship. Debby had been pretty scared about entering the Indiana State Fair. But "the judge was awfully nice," Debbie said. "He didn't scare me like some judges do. He came up and talked friendly-like." That was the warmest memory she had of that day.

At three, Debby's Orphy won the Reserve Grand Championship in the halter class. She had been bred by then. When she was six months pregnant, Debby's Orphy was hit by a car and killed. All the promise gone, too grown up and needing money for college, Debby had to live without another horse. She has a quiet smile and a kind way about her, even when she talks about the mare. One wonders if she would be as remarkable a person if she hadn't lost something so precious and overcome the loss in her heart.

There's not a rider who hasn't taken his spills. Where else can you make a fool of yourself so completely as in a show ring? It is bad enough to have a horse dump you, but to do it in public is humiliating. Yet again and again riders face this kind of defeat and go on to ride again. Small wonder the

There's always the thrill of a jump well done, and a horse who soars and cares.

If you find an artist with that special talent to catch the essence of your horse, the show world you know will be yours to remember all your life. *Oil painting by Patty Powers.*

audience cheers so loudly when a rider remounts and takes his last fence. Nor is it a small thing after landing in the dust to get up, climb back in the saddle, and gather yourself together, shaken though you may be, and ride at a fence without a moment to recover.

Tibby Hunt put her finger on what is, to me, the finest part of showing. "You get to know yourself," she said. "You learn your temperament, the kind of person you really are. You may not like what you see. It's hard to change your attitude, your disposition, even. It is especially difficult when you have so many variables to deal with, ones over which you have no control. The variables aren't constant. Take your horse, for example. He may be the kind who learns only from kindness. If you have a temper, you are going to have to change or you won't be able to train your horse. You may have to teach yourself patience and more patience." This kind of self-discipline is what makes riders. It also makes fine people.

In silhouette at nightime, the camera captures the eagerness and anticipation that can be spellbinding at a show.

Terms Horsemen Use*

"A" RATING: The highest rating of an AHSA Show. (See chapter 7.)

AHSA: American Horse Shows Association. Shows are run in accordance with its rules. You have to be a member and have permission from them to run an AHSA Show. It sets up the yearly show schedule, licenses judges, stewards, and other officials. It runs Medal Classes and totals points for Horse of the Year Award. Address: 527 Madison Avenue, New York, N. Y. 10022.

AHSA HUNTER SEAT MEDAL CLASS: See chapter 7.

AMATEUR: A rider over eighteen who does not ride professionally (professionals are paid).

AMATEUR-OWNER: See chapter 7.

AMATEUR-OWNER HUNTER STAKE: See chapter 7.

APPOINTMENT CLASS: The rider does not need to be an amateur or a member of a recognized hunt as he must be for the Corinthian Hunter Class. He must wear hunting attire—so must his horse. The AHSA rule book takes nearly three pages to describe the correct appointments.

ARC: At a normal pace, when jumping, a horse will "stand back" slightly more than the height of a jump and land the same distance away. On a spread, he will stand back about the height of the first element and land away the height of the last. On a three-and-a-half to four-foot fence he will make an eight-or nine-foot arc.

ASPCA: The American Society of Prevention of Cruelty to Animals holds a horsemanship class for junior riders. Performance under saddle counts half, the other half is judged on performance over fences. This class is often called the Maclay after the family who has given the trophy for the winner.

"B" RATING: The second highest rating given an AHSA show. Class ribbons are worth fewer points toward the Horse of the Year Award than for

---

* Also see chapter 7 for a more extensive coverage of show terms.

an "A" show, but are still double those won in a "C" show.

BALANCING YOUR HORSE (FOR JUMPING): Accentuating his weight toward his haunches.

"C" RATING: The AHSA rating given to Local recognized shows. A "C" show is anything less than a "B" rating. It usually lasts only one day. Prize money and the number of classes are less than in higher-rated shows.

CAVALLETTI: A series of bars, sometimes constructed with crisscrossed ends to raise them several inches above the ground. They are set a horse's stride apart and are used to train him to lengthen and shorten his stride, to take an even stride, and to make a correct approach to a fence. Set the bars five to six feet apart for a trot. Set them ten and a half to twelve feet three inches apart for a canter stride.

CAVALLETTO: Singular for cavalletti; one of the bars used in making up a cavalletti.

CHAMPIONSHIPS: In Hunter and Jumper divisions, championships are awarded on points. Only the first four ribbons in each class count. Normal points are five for blue, three for red, two for yellow, one for white ribbons.

CHANGE OF HAND: Change of lead.

(The) Chronicle of the Horse: A publication that covers news of the horse world including shows. (Berryville, Virginia 22611).

CONFORMATION HUNTER: See chapter 7.

DRESSAGE: The art form of riding when it is correctly performed. The training of a horse in dressage includes more than learning and obedience. It becomes fitness of mind and body, a unity of rider and horse. It is balance and coordination. Mental attitudes and physical conditioning go hand in hand, as horse and rider progress together. A rider develops feeling and the sense of timing. The classical exercises of dressage are extensions of the natural movements of a horse, although, in a performance for an audience, they seem much more. The basis of dressage that develops the fullest use of a horse's mind and muscles underlies all fine riding. Not a horseman goes over an obstacle who has not taught his horse some basic dressage, no matter what term he may call it. An understanding of dressage will improve the quality of riding and the efforts of any horse or rider who accepts its discipline. In competition, dressage is performed in a small white ring, but it may be used extensively to improve the ability of any horse to carry his rider. The performance of some of the beginning exercises of dressage are required in equitation classes. It is a demanding, difficult, and exciting form of riding. (The most comprehensive book I have found on dressage is Dressage, by Henry Wynmalen.)

ELIMINATION (IN HUNTER CLASS): For third refusal, jumping an obstacle before it is reset, going off course, bolting from the ring, jumping an obstacle not included in the course, horse or rider falling.

EQUITATION: Equitation classes are judged on the rider's performance rather than the horse's. They are also called Horsemanship classes. (See also chapter 7.)

FEI: Federation Equestre International. An internation counterpart of the AHSA. It oversees international competition. In some shows you will find classes run according to FEI rules.

GREEN HUNTER: See chapter 7.

GREEN HUNTER PONY: See chapter 7.

GREEN WORKING HUNTER: See chapter 7.

HACK: See chapter 7.

HANDS: A horse is measured by hands from the withers to the ground. A hand is four inches.

HANDY HUNTER: A horse who is good in trappy country. Courses for handy hunters must have a couple changes of direction and at least one combination. A horse may have to trot over a fence and lead over one.

HOGBACK: A fence with three rails, the middle one higher than the other two.

HORSE OF THE YEAR: The award given by the AHSA in each division to the horse who accumulates the most points during the year. The show year runs from December 1 to November 30. (Also see Chapter 7.)

HORSEMANSHIP CLASSES: Equitation classes.

HOT HORSE: Eager, spirited.

HUNTER PONY: See chapter 7.

HUNTER UNDER SADDLE: See chapter 7.

IN AND OUT: Two fences that represent a natural barrier that a horse first jumps into and then must manage to jump out of. A fence on either side of a country lane made an in and out, even though the hunters jumped out of one field and into the next. A one stride in and out is usually twenty-four-feet. (It may run twenty-one to twenty-four-feet and still be thought of as one natural stride.) A two-stride in and out will be thirty-six-feet. (It can run thirty-one to thirty-nine-feet.) You can also have a no-stride in and out for schooling.

INTERMEDIATE JUMPER: See chapter 7.

INTERMEDIATE RIDER: See chapter 7.

JUMP: A horse will jump, a rider will jump, over a fence or obstacle. Sometimes the fence itself is called a jump.

JUMPER DIVISION: See chapter 7.

JUMPING ORDER: It is posted at shows. It is rotated for the different classes. Usually a fourth of the list is shifted each time to the top of the list, but a show committee may rotate it in any systematic way.

JUNIOR HUNTER: See chapter 7.

JUNIOR JUMPER: See chapter 7.

JUNIOR RIDER: You must be under eighteen at the beginning of the show year. A rider who has not reached his eighteenth birthday by January first is considered seventeen throughout the year.

KNOCK-DOWN: Your horse knocks a portion of a fence hard enough to make it fall. Officially it means the fence has been made lower by something you or your horse did to it. If you narrow the width of a spread without lowering it, it is not a knock-down.

LIMIT: See chapter 7.

LOCAL CLASS: Entrance is limited in territory by the show's management.

LOCAL HUNTER CLASSES: See chapter 7.

LOCAL SHOWS: See chapter 7.

MACLAY: See ASPCA.

MADISON SQUARE GARDEN: A horseman who says, "I rode in the Garden," means he rode at the big fall show in Madison Square Garden in New York City. There are other top shows also. Currently, the AHSA medals finals are held at the Pennsylvania National Horse Show at Harrisburg. The Maclay finals are held at Madison Square Garden's National Horse Show each fall.

MAIDEN: See chapter 7.

MARTINGALES: Their use is optional over jumps and in equitation classes requiring both jumping and hacking. They are not allowed in equitation classes in which you don't jump. In an equitation class that has both jumping and hacking, a rider is permitted to remove his martingale when going from one phase to another.

MEDAL CLASS: See chapter 7.

MODEL CLASS: See chapter 7.

NOVICE: See chapter 7.

OBSTACLE: A fence, ditch, or other object a horse must jump. The term is used interchangeably with fence.

ON THE FLAT: Classes in which there is no jumping—no fences. They include pleasure horse, hack, under saddle, and some equitation classes.

OPEN: A class in which any rider may enter, whether he is professional or amateur, no matter how many ribbons he or his horse has won. In a working hunter or conformation hunter division, the word *open* is often replaced by *regular* (a regular working hunter).

OPEN JUMPER: See chapter 7.

OWNERS' CLASSES: Every contestant is an amateur and the rider is the owner of the horse (or the rider may also be a member of the rider's immediate family, or the prize list may make exceptions).

OXER: A fence with two vertical parts separated by a short distance. A square oxer has two elements of exactly the same height so that the horse's eye does not pick up the second part until he is in the air.

PHA: The Professional Horsemen's Association. The PHA holds horse shows and is especially interested in young riders. It was founded to help professional horsemen in need.

POLING: A pole or bamboo cane no thicker than a man's wrist that is taped to prevent splitting is held *in front* of a fence. It raps the forelegs and hind legs on the upward curve. It is used to help a horse who has become careless to realize the actual height of a fence and to take off in time. It must be done carefully and by someone experienced in its use. The best discussion I have seen on the subject is in William Stenikraus's book, *Riding and Jumping*. The actual method is described well by Rodney Jenkins in *Showing Your Horse* by Harlan C. Abbey.

PONIES UNDER SADDLE: Are ridden only by junior exhibitors. (A pony may be entered as a jumper in the jumper division; in that case he could be ridden by any rider.)

PONY: A pony is any horse or pony who is 14.2 hands or less. Your horse may not qualify as *both* a horse and a pony in the same show. (See chapter 7.)

POST ENTRIES: Any entry made after the advertised closing date for the show.

PRELIMINARY JUMPER: See chapter 7.

PROFESSIONAL: Someone who breeds, buys, sells, or boards horses; who is paid for schooling, riding, driving, or teaching; who is employed to ride or drive at a horse show; who is paid for the use of his name or photograph.

QUALIFIED HUNTER: See chapter 7.

RECOGNIZED SHOW: Shows run by members of the AHSA. The classes are not limited to those in the rule book. (See chapter 7.)

REGULAR HUNTER: See chapter 7.

REGULAR MEMBER SHOWS: See chapter 7.

RESERVE CHAMPIONSHIP: See chapter 7.

RIBBONS: First—blue; second—red; third—yellow; fourth—white; fifth—pink; sixth—green; seventh—purple; eighth—brown; ninth—gray; tenth—light blue.

RUB: Ticking a fence while jumping without knocking it down.

THE RULE BOOK: Is published by the American Horse Shows Association. You must be a member to get the rule book.

RUNOUT: Your horse goes outside a fence, avoids it. It is considered a disobedience and is a major fault.

SCARLET: A red hunt jacket, but you never say the word *red*. The color is scarlet or pink.

SHOW AGE: The age you were on January first of the current year. For show purposes that is your age throughout the year.

SILVER MEDAL: See chapter 7.

STAKE CLASS: The important class in a division—usually the money-winning class. At most shows it is the last class offered in a division.

STARTING LINE: (For jumper classes) must be at least twelve feet from the first obstacle and twenty-four feet after the last one.

STRIDE: You usually figure a normal stride for a horse at a canter is twelve feet. When he is moving slowly or on a turn at a canter on a jumper course, he will take a nine-foot stride.

SWEEPSTAKES: A class in which some or all of the money from entry fees is divided among the winners.

TESTS 1-17 FOR EQUITATION CLASSES: AHSA tests for riding skill. They may increase in number and be changed. A judge may ask for tests other than these if he wishes. Class specifications explain which tests will be used.

1. Back.
2. Gallop and pull up.
3. Figure eight at a trot demonstrating change of diagonals.
4. Figure eight at a canter with simple change of lead. (You may trot or walk a couple of steps at center of eight to change lead.)

5. Jump a low fence at a walk, a trot, a canter.
6. Pull up between fences. (You are asked to stop in front of a fence, not in the middle of a combination.)
7. Jump fences on a figure-eight course.
8. Ride without stirrups. (This can even mean over fences.)
9. Dismount and mount.
10. Jump a serpentine course, demonstrating a change of lead at each change of direction.
11. Figure eight at canter on correct lead demonstrating a flying change of lead.
12. Change leads down center of ring demonstrating simple change of lead.
13. Execute a serpentine at a trot or canter with simple or flying change of lead. (A series of left and right half circles off center of an imaginary line where correct diagonal or lead change must be shown.)
14. Ride a strange horse or change horses.
15. Canter on the counter lead (the outside lead on a circle).
16. Half turn on the forehand and/or on the haunches.
17. Demonstrate a ride of approximately one minute. Judge must be told beforehand what you are planning to do.

TOUCH CLASSES: See chapter 7.

UNDER A FENCE: A horse who comes too close to a fence for his takeoff is said to get under his fence.

UNRECOGNIZED SHOW: A show that is not run under the authority of the American Horse Shows Association. Points won here do not count toward the Horse of the Year Award. It will not affect your horse's green status. There will be no Medals Classes. Competition is easier than in recognized shows. You may use an unrecognized show as a schooling show.

USET: United States Equestrian Team. An USET Equitation class is for junior riders. Tryouts for the team are at its headquarters in Gladstone, New Jersey, or at designated places and times around the United States.

VERTICAL FENCE: A fence that is straight up and down, or nearly so, such as a wall. A horse must go high to jump over it. In a jumper course you will mentally classify fences as vertical or spread, depending on the kind of arc your horse has to make to get over them. A horse needs collection and to be on his hocks for a vertical fence. Short strides in the approach help.

WORKING HUNTER: See chapter 7.

Index